Fields of the Fatherless

Cornie,
Praying this
novel blesses you!
Elaine Marie Cooper
Phil 1:6

By Elaine Marie Cooper

FIELDS OF THE FATHERLESS BY ELAINE MARIE COOPER
Published by Lighthouse Publishing of the Carolinas
2333 Barton Oaks Dr., Raleigh, NC, 27614

ISBN 9781938499920
Copyright © 2013 by Elaine Marie Cooper
Cover design by The Killion Group, www.TheKillionGroupInc.com
Cover Photography: Heather Johnson
Book design by Reality Info Systems, www.realityinfo.com

Available in print from your local bookstore, online, or from the publisher at:
www.lighthousepublishingofthecarolinas.com

For more information on this book and the author visit:
http://www.elainemariecooper.com

Brought to you by the creative team at LighthousePublishingoftheCarolinas.com:
Alycia W. Morales, Brian Cross, Reality Info Systems, Rowena Kuo

Library of Congress Cataloging-in-Publication Data
Cooper, Elaine Marie.
Fields of the Fatherless/ Elaine Marie Cooper 1st ed.
Printed in the United States of America

Dedication

This book is dedicated to the memory of three patriots of the United States Navy who lost their lives on a training mission conducted in the state of Washington on March 11, 2013.

The aircrew members of VAQ 129 were:

LCDR Alan Patterson

LTJG Valerie Delaney

LTJG William McIlvaine III

Brave warriors continue to give the ultimate sacrifice to maintain freedom for the United States of America.

Acknowledgments

Special thanks to: Former Administrator Faith Ferguson at The Arlington Historical Society; my husband, Steve Cooper; Eddie Jones, Publisher at Lighthouse Publishing of the Carolinas; Alycia Morales, Editor; Lisa J. Lickel, friend and editor; Darin Tschopp, oxen expert at Colonial Williamsburg; Shad Clymer, D.V.M.; and fellow members of Colonial American Christian Writers, especially Joan Hochstetler, Lisa Norato, and Carrie Fancett Pagels. Thank you all for your help and for believing in this story. And to all my friends and family that have been so supportive and encouraging, I am eternally grateful. Special thanks to my Lord and Saviour, Jesus Christ, from whom all blessings flow.

Remove not the old landmark; and enter not into the fields of the fatherless:
For their redeemer is mighty; he shall plead their cause with thee.

Proverbs 23:10-11

Preface

Betsy Russell could not discern if the sweat on her palms was from her own fear or from the intensity of Anna's pain. Either source seemed a sufficient cause of the slippery pool of moisture.

Betsy, the only daughter of Jason Russell, trembled at the events occurring outside on the nearby road as well as in the birthing room. She intertwined her fingers with those of her sister-in-law so tightly that Anna's labor pains seemed to course through her own arms.

Anna screamed as a contraction gripped her swollen belly. Betsy clung to her as if she could take away the pain with the pressure of her grip. But before the pain ebbed, another sonorous blast of cannon fire echoed from hundreds of rods down the hill. The concussion reverberated throughout the house, and the walls shuddered along with the women's nerves. Even the midwife, normally a pillar of calm, turned pale.

Betsy desperately fought back fearful tears.

Why did Father not come with us?

She remembered his comforting hand on her shoulder the night he first said he was meeting with the patriot committee. He smiled at her then. All seemed as it should be with the world. But that seemed so long ago …

Another round of explosives elicited uncontrollable shivering.

Where is he now when I need his reassuring presence? Dear Lord, protect him.

The women in the room jumped when an enormous volley of musket fire rattled from the direction of Concord Road. Betsy doubted the pain-filled screams she heard were only in her imagination.

Father in heaven, this cannot be happening. How did we get to this terrible place? Dear Lord, help us.

THREE MONTHS EARLIER, JANUARY 1775
MENOTOMY VILLAGE, MASSACHUSETTS

1

The patter of rain has ceased. The sun has shown again! Were it possible that the brightness of the day would illuminate the minds of men and cause them to ponder peace? Dare I dream of such revelation in men's hearts? Or must I relinquish my dreams to the storms threatening ahead? I pray for clouds that only threaten rain without the expected deluge—clouds that only taunt us without intent to harm.
I pray 'tis so ... I pray I shall live to see my future. And my children's.

~ Diary of Betsy Russell, 14 January 1775

A sharp report of musket fire startled Betsy Russell so that she nearly pricked her finger. Setting aside the smock she was sewing, she rose from her chair and peered out of the small window panes.

Opening her mouth in protest, she tried appearing casual with her words.

"So, Father teaches Noah how to fire a musket." Her voice was steady, but she couldn't keep a scowl from betraying her irritation.

The men all learn to defend themselves whilst the women sew. Will a sewing needle protect us from our enemies?

Her mother raised her eyes above the reading glasses perched on her nose. She worked on her own sewing project, a new gown for the grandchild that her daughter-in-law Anna carried.

"Is it so strange that he should teach your brother how to use a firelock?" Betsy's mother, Elizabeth, said.

"Nay. I vow most lads of twelve have learned the skill. 'Tis just ..." Frustrated, she blurted out, "'Tis just that I wish to learn as well. Why, pray, do the lads learn to shoot at the marks whilst the women sew?"

Her mother set the linen material in her lap and sighed with an air of exasperation. "Betsy, each of us has our place and our occupation.

Yours is to tend to the home. The men must protect the home. That is their duty, and 'tis not always a pleasant one at that."

"Nay, perhaps not pleasant, yet ..." Betsy grimaced. "Yet, what if the men are gone? How will we women protect our homes? Must we bow to the evil devices of an enemy without so much as a fowling piece to defend ourselves?"

Elizabeth was silent for a moment before answering. "There are some women who can fire a musket, if need be."

Betsy gaped. "Mother! You know the manner of shooting a musket? But why—"

Elizabeth held up her hand. Betsy knew better than to speak further.

"Betsy, your father vowed the day you were born that you would be protected so that you might grow to bear your own children." Her mother's mouth trembled as she drew it into a thin line across her face. "Our first daughter, Elizabeth, you know—she was with us far too few years. Only seven."

Once again I am haunted by the "other Elizabeth."

Betsy regretted her thoughts as she saw her mother's eyes glisten.

Forgive my foul musings, Lord. Soften my tongue.

"I know, Mother. But my sister in heaven never had a chance to be old enough to hold a musket. That is not why she died."

Elizabeth turned her moist eyes toward her daughter. "Nay, Betsy, that is not why she died. But handling a firelock is dangerous business. You remember what happened with that poor Mrs. Fessenden nearly four years ago. 'Twas the hand of God that protected that dear infant sitting in her lap when that careless boy shot that young mother. The worst tragedy—"

"I remember it well, Mother. And I'm quite aware of the danger, but there are other dangers as well. Father says the Minutemen now muster three times a week. He meets with the town committee every week, even though 'tis against the British Parliament for colonists to do so. Father says we may go to war ..."

Elizabeth held up her hand again. "I vow, Betsy, we must not speak of this. I cannot bear the thought." Elizabeth's fingers gripped the linen so tightly while she sewed that Betsy observed a row of wrinkles in the cloth.

Mother cannot acknowledge what is so obvious. Her heart still grieves so for her lost children. Does she not consider that we may all die if we are not prepared? Lord, I pray that You help her to understand with Your gentle Spirit. Help us to be ready, I pray.

Betsy concentrated on her sewing project. "I'm sorry, Mother. Please forgive me speaking of such things." She smiled as she glanced apologetically toward her. "I do not wish to grieve you with my speech."

Her mother shook her head. "Think no more of it." Staring at Betsy's project, she nodded. "I see Josiah's smock is nearly complete."

"Aye, I think 'twill fit him nicely for Sabbath Day." Betsy held up the child-size shirt with long sleeves and a neatly sewn collar—a perfect fit for her seven-year-old nephew from New Hampshire. "I wonder how long he'll keep this linen so white." Both women grinned.

Such misbehavior a young boy can get into! But I treasure him so— dirt and all.

"Not long enough, I daresay." Elizabeth glanced toward the window of the main room. "Since you've completed your project, refresh yourself outdoors. 'Tis finally a sun-filled day after all the rain we've had. The sunshine will lift your spirits."

Betsy glanced across the room at Pumpkin the cat, who lay curled up in a ray of sunshine on the floor.

"Pumpkin is certainly content with this weather."

Standing, she stretched out her arms with relief. "It has been such a strange winter. So little snow and so much rain. And now, a sunny, cool day in January." She shook her head. "I've never seen such a winter in my eighteen years."

Her mother laughed. "Not so many years. There are odd seasons such as this over time. At my age, there's many a story to tell of strange weather. Someday, you can tell your own children about this strange winter that was not a winter at all."

My own children …

Betsy smiled despite the lingering ache that pinched her heart. Sighing, she lifted her woolen cloak from the hook on the wall near the door.

"Have you heard anything from Amos, Betsy?"

The young woman froze in her steps. "Nay, Mother. It has been quite some time since you've inquired about him."

"I know that it grieved your heart when he joined the Sons of Liberty in Boston."

Betsy glanced at the floor before meeting her mother's softened eyes. "Aye. But that was a year ago. I daresay he was more passionate about his country than me."

Adjusting the hood of her cloak over her mobcap, Betsy turned the handle of the wooden door and stepped outdoors. She deeply breathed in the sweet-smelling air and allowed the gentle breeze to sweep thoughts of Amos farther away from her heart.

2

Strolling toward her father and Noah, Betsy hugged her cloak around her arms. Although a warmer January than most, the moist chill in the air sent a shiver creeping up her arms.

The soft wool comforted Betsy, sparking thoughts of her father tucking her under her quilt at night. But that occurred long ago when she was small, long before there was talk of war.

She listened as her father patiently instructed her twelve-year-old brother.

"'Tis important you add just enough powder into the pan to cause a spark but not so much as to cause a flame." Jason Russell turned toward his daughter and grinned. "Your brother Noah is becoming a man now."

Betsy's heart warmed at the proud expression on her father's countenance. In the winter sunlight, streaks of silver hair wrapped like a shimmering crown around his head, the long strands pulled back into a queue. He chuckled as he readjusted the butt of the wooden stock against Noah's shoulder. "Hold it just so, lad."

Noah's long fingers gripped the stock and pointed it toward the mark on a far oak tree along the edge of the woods. With his thumb, he cocked the lock and then squeezed the trigger with a steady finger.

Betsy jumped at the sharp report. As her father glanced briefly her way, she smiled in an attempt to cover her nervousness.

"Well done, Noah. Are you all right, Betsy? Perhaps ye're standing too close."

"I am fine, Father."

Father resumed teaching Noah the art of musketry, but his expression grew less jovial. "Lad, the most important thing to remember about your firelock is that it is a weapon never to be trifled with. Never let folly lead you to foolishness."

Noah pointed the musket toward the ground. Yesterday he had the eyes of a child. Today, his visage bore the maturity of one who understood that he held the power of life and death in his grip.

"I understand, Father." Noah met his eyes with a steady gaze.

"Good lad." Father patted his shoulder. "And always remember—this land you're standin' on was settled by my great-grandfather. Russells have sweat over this soil for many a year. A musket can ensure it remains our home, no matter the intentions of any other."

Like King George and his Parliament. Betsy scowled.

Mother's urgent voice drew their attention toward the house. She had her hands upon Josiah's shoulders. "Jason! Josiah bears a sty in his eye."

Father's weary expression sagged as he sighed. "I'll take him to the smith."

Betsy rested her hand on her father's arm. "No need. I'll take him."

He smiled. "Thank you, lass."

Trudging back toward the house, Betsy noticed the small, reddened swelling under Josiah's right eye. "Let us be off, young man." Grinning at her nephew, she guided him back to the abode to get his woolen jacket.

Betsy turned around briefly to watch her father and brother pointing toward the target and likely discussing the best strategies to hit their mark. Her brow furrowed as she watched her father limp painfully over to the only outdoor furniture in the meadow behind their two-story home—a chair.

If only his foot had healed properly.

Ten years earlier, the doctor had told Betsy's mother that Jason might never walk again after a crushing fracture from a plowing accident. Betsy's father would abide no such predictions, however. It took him several months, but he did indeed get upright again of his own power, although the awkwardness in his gait remained, as well as occasional bouts of intense pain. Physical suffering reflected in his eyes. Over the years, Betsy watched as the strain in his features increased along with wrinkles in his face.

Poor Father.

She turned back toward Josiah, who now wore a woolen coat that his grandmother buttoned with her knobby fingers. After closure was complete, Elizabeth patted the boy on the head. "There now, Josiah. Mr. Watson shall take care of that sty in no time. Go on with you."

They began the mile-long walk on the dirt-covered pathway known as Concord Road. *To think I used to enjoy the journey to Boston.*

Even going a short distance—closer to General Gage and his army of the arrogant British king's soldiers—put tension in Betsy's stride.

What is their intent?

After the heavy taxation was levied on the tea coming into Boston, the Sons of Liberty had thrown the cargo from three ships into Boston Harbor. That was over a year ago, yet King George still wished to starve the citizens of Boston into submission. What the ruler in England did not count on was the determination of the colonists to fight back. The rest of the colonies rallied to supply food to the people in the city. When one colony suffered from parliamentary dictates, they all suffered, her father had said.

Betsy heard her nephew whine from the pain as he rubbed his eye.

"You mustn't poke at it, Josiah. That will make it worse."

"But it itches so."

She pitied the boy's tone. Betsy reached for his hand to help him on the walk to the blacksmith's shop just across Menotomy River, but Josiah pulled his hand away. "I'm not a child, Aunt Betsy. I can walk by myself."

Betsy smiled at his indignant attitude. "I do apologize, Josiah. I forgot that you are no longer a young child of six." She found it difficult to squelch her laugh.

The boy covered his sore eye with one hand while looking up at his aunt. "'Tis well that none of my friends were here to see you." He shook his head in disgust.

"I must be more careful. I would not wish to embarrass you in front of your mature friends."

"Are you laughing at me, Aunt Betsy?" He stopped in the road and looked up at her.

She put one hand on his shoulder and looked at him. "I'll not make fun of your desire to be grown up, Josiah. I did not give it two seconds' thought before grabbing your hand, and I am sorry. Now, let's be on our way to Mr. Watson's."

They resumed their walk. Still covering his sore eye, the boy looked up sideways. "Aunt Betsy, what is a mote?"

"A moat is a river of water surrounding a castle. It is meant to keep a king's enemies away from his home."

"Oh." He squinted his good eye in confusion. "Then why would there be a river of water in one's eye?"

Now it was Betsy's turn to be confused. "Pray, what do you mean, Josiah?"

"Well, Reverend Cooke said, 'And why beholdest thou the mote that is in thy brother's eye ...'" The boy paused, appearing deep in thought. "I cannot remember the rest."

"Ah, I see. Reverend Cooke was referring to a speck of sawdust like the fine pieces of wood at the sawmill. He was referring to the Scripture that speaks of taking care of our own large sins before we go looking for the small transgressions of others. The motes." She looked with pride at her nephew. "'Tis a blessing to know you are listening to the reverend on Sabbath Day, Josiah. Your father will be quite pleased to hear."

"I miss Father. He *will* be back for me in spring, will he not?"

"Aye. He'll not forget you ... much as I would wish to keep you with us." She gave him a quick hug, but he squirmed away.

"Aunt Betsy! The Minutemen will see you! I do *not* wish to be embarrassed."

"Do forgive me, Josiah." She glanced at the nearby green, observing the militia unit of fifty men from Menotomy Village practicing their drills in preparation for war. Betsy's expression fell as a chill swirled its way underneath her woolen cloak.

Josiah had stopped walking, apparently forgetting his sore eye. He fixed his gaze on the men who practiced formations, pointing their muskets at imaginary enemies, while another group honed their targeting skills. Every male from their town who was sixteen years or older participated in the drills three times a week. The older men and the infirm—like Betsy's father—were exempted from this duty. She knew that were her father not lame, he would muster with these troops, despite his advanced age of fifty-eight. He had bemoaned his lame foot on more than one occasion, declaring his desire to fight the "bloody 'backs."

Betsy shivered. "Come on, Josiah. Your grandsire wishes us to visit the smith."

As if suddenly remembering the sty, Josiah winced and covered his eye again with one hand.

Approaching the wooden bridge, Betsy heard the sound of the swollen Menotomy River, full from the persistent rains. At first, the rushing water reminded Betsy of the first time she and Amos kissed when they walked hand-in-hand by this same river. But the surging water soon filled her with fear as its pace instilled anxiety. Its intense beat coursed through her veins, as if the churning flow were the footsteps of a charging army. Her steps quickened as she tightened her cloak around herself.

The two strode in silence for several rods before Josiah spoke.

"Perhaps we need a moat."

Betsy narrowed her eyes. "We need some sawdust?"

"Nay—the other moat that you told me about. A river of water surrounding Grandsire's house. To keep the bloody 'backs away."

"Josiah! Your mother would be appalled to hear you speak that way."

His face turned crimson. "I'm sorry, Aunt Betsy. A river to keep the … umm … regulars away from the house. Just like the king has around his castle." He looked at her with one hopeful eye, the other hidden behind small fingers.

She smiled at his childish solution. "T'would be a fine strategy, Josiah. But, I vow, not even the whole ocean has kept the king's troops away from America. I fear that even a moat would not protect us. I think we must ask God to be our defender against so powerful a foe—and trust our brave militia to stand against them. We're in safe hands." She squeezed his shoulder for reassurance.

I wish I felt so confident.

"There now, we are at Mr. Watson's shop."

The forge belonging to Jacob Watson was a three-sided, barn-like structure, covered with a shingled roof but completely open on one side. Attached to the side of the exterior of his house, it stood just one story tall. In the winter, the fire from the smithy was sufficient to keep warm; in summer, the heat would be unbearable were it enclosed. The massive amounts of smoke and steam needed freedom to escape the work area that was in near-constant use, save Sabbath Day. Only then did the forge lay dormant.

Jacob Watson, like most blacksmiths, was a pillar in his community, providing the many necessities of nearly every man, woman, and child. There was nary a wheel piece, saddle fastener, nor kitchen tool in Menotomy that had not felt the blow of his forceful hammer as he forged the iron and steel implements of everyday life.

This year, Betsy knew that Jacob's most-requested items were the tools of war: swords and knives for the Minutemen and horseshoes for their mounts. None of these items were out in the open, Betsy noticed. She knew that, were he discovered by the king's army, he would be hung for providing aid to the militia. She gulped at the thought of her friend hanging on the end of a British rope.

The hissing sound of steam greeted Betsy as Jacob plunged a hot bar of iron into water to cool it down.

Betsy forced a friendly smile. "Good day, Mr. Watson."

He turned at the sound of her voice.

"I fear my nephew here has acquired a sty under his eye, and father requested I take him to you."

Jacob revealed a set of white teeth in the middle of his soot-covered face. He placed his burly hands on his hips. His heavy, leather apron squeaked as it rubbed against his massive chest and belly. "Well, now, is that so, young Mr. Josiah?"

The boy nodded and covered his eye while scrunching his face.

"Well, lad, I'll be with ye soon enough. Why don't ya come hither and see this axe head I'm forgin'?"

Josiah hesitated, but Betsy urged him forward. "'Tis fine, Josiah. He'll not let you get too close."

The boy walked slowly toward Jacob and watched with rapt attention. The smith gripped the piece of iron with a large metal tong and heated it until it was red, then beat it with several blows of the hammer. After the iron submitted to the tool, Jacob plunged the hot piece into the slack tub filled with water, where steam surrounded the worker and his small audience of one. Jacob repeated the process, stoking the fire that he allowed Josiah to look at closely.

Between the steam and the smoke, Josiah's eyes began to water. The boy must not have noticed, because he never wiped the moisture off his face. When Jacob had completed the axe head, he set his tools on the anvil.

"Now then. Where be this sty your grandsire spoke of?"

Josiah blinked several times and first pointed to one eye, then the other. "I think it was this one, but I am not certain."

Betsy covered her mouth to keep from laughing. She observed the blacksmith gently push the boy's head back. "Well, well. Everything looks well enough." Turning toward Betsy, he winked. "Looks like the steam and smoke did the job right thorough."

Josiah's eyes narrowed. "What happened, Aunt Betsy?"

"Looks like the sty has opened and gone away, Josiah. Mr. Watson is quite the sty doctor, is he not?" She picked up his long queue of hair and tugged on it gently. "You are well enough, indeed."

As if forgetting he was ever in discomfort, Josiah ran out toward the bridge. "I want to throw rocks in the river."

"Don't get too close to the water."

"I won't, Aunt Betsy."

Betsy paused for a moment while watching her nephew play. She felt the urge to speak to Mr. Watson about her fears, but she did not know where to begin. Clutching her cloak, she smiled awkwardly and looked at the ground.

Jacob put his hands on his hips. "Somethin' weighin' on yer heart, Miss Russell?"

She took in a hurried breath and gathered her courage. "Aye, Mr. Watson. Pray, forgive me for asking you to bear this burden of mine, but there's no one at home to confide my fears to. Father just keeps telling me 'twill be all right, he'll watch out for me. And Mother ... she ne'er wishes to discuss the possibility that we may go to war with England. It seems the very thought constricts her words." Betsy's voice trailed off.

Thoughts of impending war dampened her all-too-brief, lighthearted respite.

I wish there were more jovial moments in my life.

Jacob soberly glanced at the dirt floor of the shop, then looked up. "'Tis difficult for parents to speak of such things to their child, Miss Russell. Yer parents take much delight in their only daughter. To speak of such concerns as the loomin' war is a frightenin' talk for a mother and sire. I know. I wish I didna' have to prepare my family neither."

Betsy's eyes looked in earnest at the smith. "Mr. Watson, not speaking of the fear will not change the facts. I want to be ready. I do not wish to be unprepared. My father says he'll protect us, but what if he's gone with the militia? Then what? 'Tis certain, I have no way to defend myself or my family."

She clutched her cloak with tight fingers and felt her heart pounding through the wool.

Jacob's eyes softened and crinkled with his warm smile. "I know your father does not wish you to carry a musket, lass. 'Tis true that the men will do the fightin'." He paused and then lowered his voice. "But the women are always in danger as well." He inhaled sharply and stared at the sky for a moment before he turned toward her. "Wait here."

Clomping with heavy boots across the length of his shop, he stooped down toward a large wooden box. After sorting through several pieces of clanking metal, he stopped when he found the object of his quest. Holding up a small, shining piece, he straightened with a grunt and stretched his back for a moment before walking over to her.

His eyes held a conspiratorial glint as they narrowed in his face. Mr. Watson glanced around and kept his voice low. "I made this knife some years ago. A neighbor wanted it for his growin' son, but the lad died before the father ever came to pick up the piece. 'Tis somewhat small for most men, but it would fit your grip. See what ya think."

The smith handed Betsy the steel blade, expertly forged and sharp as any saber. It was smaller than most hunting knives, but it fit Betsy's hand as if it were made just for her. She turned it back and forth, admiring its glimmer in the waning winter sunlight.

"'Tis perfect. I don't know what to say, Mr. Watson. I'm certain this must cost a great deal." She mentally calculated how much money she had saved from the eggs she sold to her brother's store. *I doubt I have enough to pay.* Betsy handed it back to the smith with regret. *My one chance to feel safe ...*

Instead of taking it, Mr. Watson carefully wrapped her fingers around the handle. "'Tis a gift. 'Twill make you feel safer."

Her eyes widened as she gasped. "Mr. Watson, I do not know what to say."

"Then say nothing at all, lass. This knife was not helpin' anyone sittin' in my chest. 'Twill be useful for you, to be sure." His weathered face smiled, then grew more serious. "Likely you'll never need to use it, mind you. But if someone comes at ya, wield the blade from below and point it upward under the ribs—toward the heart."

Shuddering, she forced a smile. "Thank you, sir." She squeezed his hand briefly and curtsied, then carefully placed the deadly instrument into her pocket.

Mr. Watson watched her with a slight frown. "You might wish to get a sheath to protect yourself from its sharpness."

Betsy smiled. "I already have one in mind." She curtsied again and went to meet up with Josiah, who was still casting stones into the water.

"Are ya done, Aunt Betsy? I'm cravin' some victuals."

"Aye, Josiah. I'm ready now."

I'm ready to do my part to defend us. She stood taller as she walked confidently toward home.

3

*I'm tossing and turning in my bed this night. Thoughts of Amos still
plague my spirit. Why did he have to go? And why do I still wish he
had stayed? I'll not forget his last night with me—his kisses that wanted
more than I was willing to give. He looked so angry when I refused.
Should I have said "Aye?" Could I have lived with the shame? Nay, I
could not stare at myself in the looking glass ever again without seeing
the reproach of God in my own eyes. I must sleep. 'Tis sabbath.*

~ Diary of Betsy Russell, 30 January 1775

The damp air this last day of January prompted Betsy to hug her
woolen cloak around her shoulders. Sitting in the cold, unheated
meetinghouse this Sabbath Day, she found it difficult to concentrate
on Reverend Cooke's words. She forced herself to pay attention as he
spoke about baptism.

"While we all believe baptism to be no more than a token of our
being cleansed by the blood of Christ and our solemn dedication to Him,
the mode or manner, if done in sincerity, ought not to break Christian
fellowship. It is that love and charity among Christ's disciples by which
we give the best evidence of our loving union to Him. Where there is
angry disputing, there is contention, confusion, and every evil work!"

*Angry disputing seems the order of the day. But 'tis the cause of liberty
that brings out the contention in Menotomy.*

She glanced at the pew on the left where the Shurtleif family used
to worship. It lay cold and bare, a startling reminder of the family's
loyalist sympathies. In the dark of night, they removed themselves
from this patriotic stronghold, outnumbered and unwelcome.

I hope they never return. Betsy smothered the anger in her heart, guilt overriding her patriotic sympathies. *I must guard my heart from evil.*

She recalled how her father had recently cautioned her against hatred towards the Tories. Always a man of Christian principles, he did not allow his passion for liberty to color his responsibilities to his faith. He despised cruel acts against Americans—the pillaging, food deprivations, and hangings—but he always maintained the necessity to love his enemy. His words echoed in her thoughts: "'Tis imperative to forgive, Betsy. 'Tis the Lord's command."

She sighed deeply. *Why did that seem so easy for him?*

Betsy could feel her mother's gaze. As she met Elizabeth's eyes, her parent's glance directed her back to the podium. *Mother always knows when my mind wanders.*

Trying to be attentive, she straightened herself in the pew to better focus on Reverend Cooke's words. His impassioned pleas to the congregation reverberated off the wooden walls while his upraised arm flapped the sleeve of his black robe like a waving flag.

"They who love Christ will walk in all His ordinances, blameless," shouted the reverend. Betsy's cheeks burned at the words. His sermon continued: "The true believer will follow the Lamb of God, copy His life, thankfully commemorate His death, and renew the dedication of himself to Christ at His holy table, that he may become more and more conformed to His likeness."

As Reverend Cooke completed his sermon, Thomas Cutter stood in the balcony to lead the choir in singing the closing hymn. The minister's words clung to Betsy's thoughts: "All they who love Christ will walk in all His ordinances, blameless."

I am certainly not blameless. She wrestled with so many things; her anger at Amos for leaving, hatred for the Tories and the British, discontent with her position in life. *How can I be "blameless" with so much sin in my heart? Is my soul a lost cause?*

When the song was finished, her father stepped out of their family pew, allowing his wife and children to walk ahead of him. He gripped his musket in one hand while holding the pew door open with the other.

"Thank you, Father." She gave him a half smile as she left the pew.

"Betsy."

"Aye, Father?"

"You seem heavy of heart, lass. A burden weighin' on it?"

Glancing at the wooden floor, Betsy waited to answer while the last of the congregants moved past them.

"Father, the reverend says we must be blameless if we are Christian. But … I am so filled with sin—so very flawed. And I truly hate the British. And the wretched Tories! How can they spy on their very neighbors and cause us harm?" Her eyes moistened as she earnestly sought his wisdom.

He patted her shoulder. "Betsy, do ya think that I do not wrestle with these feelings? We all do, lass. I spend some days in deep prayer as I beg God to forgive my natural instincts to hate my enemies. 'Tis your *heart* God seeks. A heart that desires to forgive and submit to His laws. Our sinful nature leads us down one road. But a heart that desires to follow His ways—that is the path that leads to God."

Her father leaned down and kissed her forehead and smiled.

"Thank you, Father."

"Jason! Jason Russell!" The voice from the open doorway caught their attention.

"Aye, Samuel, be right with ya." He placed his tricorne hat upon his head and limped toward the doorway. Mr. Whittemore followed, speaking in an earnest tone and waving his hands about.

A voice from behind drew Betsy's attention.

"Miss Russell."

Betsy faced the young farmer holding his hat. "Mr. Tidd."

Amos' best friend. She had done her best to avoid him these last months, but he had managed to find her today. Alone. She shifted her feet and moisture oozed in her palms.

He cleared his throat. "I saw ye and yer young nephew day afore last on the road near the river." His fingers shifted nervously around the edge of his woolen hat. "Our brigade was practicing drills, if ye recall."

"Aye, I do. Josiah had a sty, so Mr. Watson treated him with a dose of steam and smoke." Betsy grinned, remembering Josiah's amazement.

Zachariah Tidd paused a moment then swallowed with difficulty. "Ye're a sight to behold when ye smile, Miss Russell."

Betsy's heart sank as a strange combination of both fear and repulsion swept over her.

Her grin faded. "Oh. I did not know." She readjusted the cap on her head and nervously placed her woolen hood over the linen. "I must be goin', Mr. Tidd."

He grabbed her arm and released it as quickly. "Beg your pardon, Miss. I was just wonderin', Miss, with the war so close and all … if we have to leave to go fight, will ye think of me?"

His eyes pled with her to say "yes," but she knew that he wanted her to think of him in a way that she could not. He had long indicated to her that his feelings were more than friendship. Betsy only thought of him as little more than an acquaintance. Besides, did he want from her what Amos had sought? Was he just like his best friend?

Lord, give me the words to say.

After a long pause, she replied, "I shall think of you and all of our fine Minutemen from Menotomy. And I shall earnestly pray for everyone's safe return."

Zachariah's face fell. "Thank ye, Miss Russell. Good day." He turned on his heels and hurried out the door.

I couldn't lie to him.

But an uncomfortable remorse flooded her heart. She wished she could have said words that would please him more than a placative reply. She knew her answer pained the man, and tears welled with her regret.

Everything about war is painful.

4

I miss my friend, Sarah. There is so much we were going to do together. Meet the perfect men to marry. Have the perfect family of eight children each. Grow old together drinking tea and reminiscing like old Mother Batherick does with her friend, Mother Hawkins. But that was before Sarah took ill and died. Now I have no one to share my hopes and dreams with. No one to share my fears. I am quite alone in my fear.

~ Diary of Betsy Russell, 12 February 1775

FEBRUARY 1775

The front door slammed in the small foyer below Betsy's bedroom. Hurrying to the doorway, she cracked it open slightly to hear her father's report of his early morning meeting with the men of Menotomy.

Ever since her father had spoken with their neighbors after Sabbath service yesterday, Betsy knew trouble was afoot. Although her father would never reveal the discussion that took place at today's assembly, Betsy knew that Jason Russell always confided in his wife. A twinge of guilt for eavesdropping crept into her conscience, but she was desperate to know something—anything.

Her mother's voice rose up the stairwell where Betsy stood listening at her wooden door.

"Ye're soaked clear through with this rain, Jason." Betsy heard her mother shake the rainwater off her husband's coat, like she always did when he came inside from a storm.

"Wet clothes are the least of my worries, Elizabeth." Her father limped into the main room below. His chair scraped against the wooden floor, and Betsy envisioned him drawing close to the burning hearth.

"Three of Gage's spies were seen at Brewster's Tavern. Word has it they're scoutin' the countryside, gatherin' information."

There was a slight tremor in her mother's voice. "And what kind of information can they glean, Jason?"

"With Tories everywhere about, they can gather plenty. Our numbers of Minutemen, where we're storin' the powder and cannons. No tellin' what kind of harm they're doin' to our cause." Her father sneezed.

"Jason, you must stay out of this wretched weather before you catch your death. We do not need to battle the grippe whilst battling Gage and his troops." Her mother paused. "How did Brewster know they were spies?"

"He recognized their high-born speech. They rather stood out amongst the regular patrons there. They were dressed as surveyors, but one of Brewster's servants recognized them as belonging to Gage's troops. She had only recently come from Boston, so she was well acquainted with the king's officers. When one of them made some remark about our 'fine country around here,' Brewster's maid says, ''Tis a very fine country and we have many fine, brave men to fight for it.' That surely caught them off guard."

"Here, husband, drink this warm cider."

Her pulse throbbing, Betsy closed the door as quietly as she could. *Gage's men coming closer?* Her heart leaped into her throat.

Since her parents thought she was still asleep, she tiptoed across the room and gingerly opened her top drawer. Hidden in her silk sewing case was the gleaming metal knife that the blacksmith had given her. As she drew it out, its glistening blade shimmered more than usual from the trembling in her hands. Placing it back inside its leather sheath, Betsy tucked it inside her gown pocket, determined to carry it with her at all times.

"Betsy! Noah! Josiah! Time to awaken!" Her mother's voice rose up the steep wooden stairwell.

Lest her mother hear her reply too quickly, Betsy paused a moment before calling down in a voice that sounded falsely sleepy, "Coming, Mother."

She heard her nephew, Josiah, start to move around next door. *Noah will not awaken so easily.*

Betsy's twelve-year-old brother seemed intent upon sleeping in later and later these days. Her mother said that was common at his age, although it would not be tolerated when there was work to be done. On this rainy morning, it would be more difficult to arouse his growing frame.

Betsy splashed chilled water onto her face then glanced in the small looking glass. Although others sometimes commented on her loveliness, all Betsy could see was that her eyes appeared too close together and her lips were too large. And her hair! Why could it never curl like Polly Cutter's?

God has certainly spared me from vanity.

She sighed while spinning her waist-length locks into a knot, holding it together with wooden pins, then tucking it under her mobcap. She threw a shawl around her shoulders to keep away the damp chill. Lastly, she patted the pocket that contained her weapon. Satisfied, she squeaked across the wooden floorboards to join her family downstairs.

Passing the boys' room, she glanced inside and saw her brother still asleep. "Best get up before Mother sends Josiah to jump on your bed." Betsy smirked and carefully stepped down the uneven stairs. She heard Noah groan sleepily in his room.

Entering the main room, Betsy forced herself to smile. She kept her arms busy smoothing down her apron so the tension in her limbs would not be evident. She did not wish to reveal that she had heard her parents' conversation about the spies.

I will be brave. She inhaled deeply. *No sense in revealing my fear.* But, it was difficult to reason with her heartbeat, which persisted in thumping faster than normal. The beat pounding in her ears was unnerving.

"Corn gruel's ready, Betsy. Soon as you're finished, please go milk the cow."

"Aye, Mother."

An abrupt knock on the door startled Betsy. When she jumped, her hand knocked the tankard of cider into her trencher of gruel.

Her mother gave her a queer expression. "No matter, Betsy. Are you all right?"

How can Mother be so calm?

"I'm fine. Forgive my clumsy hands. I'll answer the door." She forced a nervous giggle and stood. Taking in a deep breath, she walked with determination toward the heavy oak door, pulled the handle, and breathed in a sigh of relief to see her older brother, Thomas.

"Thomas! No need to knock. You're family." She opened the door wider as he stepped inside and removed his hat, letting the rainwater roll off the brim.

"I did not wish to frighten anyone by suddenly opening the door. Nerves are raw these days. Is Mother home?"

"Aye, of course."

"Thomas!" Elizabeth stepped toward her son and pecked a kiss on his cheek. "What brings you out from your store on such a day? Is Anna not well?"

"'Tis naught to do with the child she carries, but her head does pain her. I thought perhaps Betsy might come and help out so Anna can rest. I must mind the storefront." He glanced hopefully at his sister.

"Of course, Thomas, I'd be glad to. Noah can milk the cow. Let me get my cloak, and I'll come forthwith."

Her mother's eyebrows furrowed. "Betsy, you must watch for strangers about."

Betsy managed to grin. "'Tis just a few rods down the road, Mother. No need to fret." She kissed both her parents.

Her father caught her hand. Worry lines etched across his forehead. "Do listen to your mother now, Betsy."

"Aye, Father." She kissed him again and squeezed his hand. "Thomas will watch out for me."

Am I really so concerned just walking down the road? Do I need someone to watch out for me? What has happened to our lives?

She threw her woolen cloak on and stepped outside onto the granite stoop. Careful to avoid puddles, she stepped around the rising pools of chilly water and allowed her brother to support one of her arms to keep her from slipping.

"Such a strange winter," she said. "Where, I pray, is that troublesome snow?"

Thomas gave a tentative laugh. "It seems to have decided to go elsewhere this year. 'Tis February, with no sign of the white flakes. I must say, I prefer this to the snowstorms."

"I do as well. I'm sorry that Anna is feeling ill."

"Her head pains her something awful today. She says it's because she's had to give up tea along with the rest of us patriots. In the past, she's always relied on her Bohea to send her headaches away."

"Cannot she have even one cup—as a medicinal?"

Thomas huffed. "Tell that to Deacon Adams—that it is merely medicinal." He shook his head. "I don't think the committee men assigned to our neighborhoods will likely accept any excuse for drinking Tory tea!"

Betsy's eyes narrowed. "I suppose not."

Arriving at the front door of her brother's store, Betsy crossed the threshold, trying to carry as little rain indoors as possible. She squeaked with wet shoes through the aisle containing milled flour, sugar loaves, and canisters of coffee beans, carefully keeping her arms down so that no moisture dripped onto the dry goods.

"I'll do my best to help Anna be comfortable, Thomas."

He smiled gratefully. "Thank you, Betsy." He began sorting through his inventory of tobacco.

After quietly opening the door to the family's living quarters, she removed her wet shoes and crossed the main room. Her sister-in-law covered her forehead with her hand as she sat on a cane chair, feet propped up on a stool.

"Hello, Betsy. Thank you for coming." Anna's voice sounded so small and strained.

"Dear Anna, would you not be more comfortable on your bed?"

"Nay, Betsy. 'Tis too cold in there. The hearth in here is far warmer."

Betsy gently pulled the quilt across her sister-in-law's swollen belly. "Let me know if I can bring you something—anything—to relieve your headache."

Anna took her hand away from her eyes for a moment and squinted painfully. "You can make me some tea!"

Betsy glanced around nervously and whispered. "Anna, please keep your voice low."

The pregnant woman groaned. "I pray, shall not even a woman with child be allowed tea when she is in distress? Next thing you know, they'll be banning wine during a birthing!" Anna nearly cried.

Betsy drew near and took her hand. "I'm so sorry. You know 'tis not to make you miserable. We can only brew our own garden herbs or drink coffee while we take a stand against the king's tax. But I know the garden leaves are not the same."

Anna's eyes overflowed with tears. "Well, let Mr. Hancock carry a child and suffer from such a headache. Then we shall see how long we must avoid drinking black tea." She wiped the moisture from her face. "I'm sorry, Betsy. You know that I am as much a patriot as you—and as much as John Hancock. But my head hurts so." She covered her eyes again with trembling fingers.

Betsy stared out the window and looked around. "Anna, what if … no, never mind."

Anna removed her hand and looked with curiosity at Betsy. "What if, what?"

Betsy licked her lips and walked back next to Anna. "What if I brewed up some Bohea … in your coffeepot? Are you brave enough to try?"

Anna smirked. "I am desperate enough to try."

Betsy gave a conspiratorial grin. "All right then. Stay here, and I'll fix you some. But you must tell me where your stash is. I know you have one."

Anna opened one eye. "Look in the bottom of the candle box on the wall."

Walking over to the wooden wall box, Betsy opened it and removed the tallow candles. She reached deeply into the pocket until she felt a cloth pouch. Pulling it out, she untied the twine drawstring and opened the small, linen sack.

"Very clever, Anna." Grinning even wider, Betsy grabbed the pewter coffee pot from the Chippendale table, sifted a few scoops of the tea leaves into the bottom of the pot, and poured hot water from the kettle into it. She set it on the small table board and sat down in a chair near Anna. As the sweet scent of tea infused the room, they breathed in the familiar, soothing aroma.

Anna closed her eyes and smiled as she leaned back. "I have missed the comforting smell."

For a moment, the two young women reveled in the tea-filled atmosphere. A sharp knock at the door interrupted their reverie.

Betsy jumped up from her chair, her breath quickening. "Who might that be on this rainy morning?"

Anna turned pale. "I know not!" She grabbed her swollen belly and sat up.

"What do I do?" Betsy wrung her hands and spoke faster than usual.

"You must answer it." Anna's eyes widened and her fingers gripped the armrests of her chair.

"Yes. I must." Betsy smoothed her linen gown and wiped her hands on her apron. Taking in a deep breath, she sauntered toward the door but tripped on a wooden floorboard. Catching herself, she grabbed her chest and closed her eyes, gasping for breath. "Dear Lord, please do not condemn us."

She forced herself to approach the door, then smiled and thrust it open. There, facing her, was Deacon John Adams.

The committeeman for our neighborhood. We are doomed!

The committeeman assigned to each neighborhood monitored every household to ensure they were supporting the patriot cause. Drinking tea was strictly forbidden.

Will I be arrested? Her heart raced and she grew dizzy.

"Mr. Adams. How pleasant to see you."

Does he see the panic in my eyes?

"Well, Miss Russell, how pleasant to see you here. I was just in the neighborhood and thought I would stop in to check on Mrs. Russell and see if there is anything she might need."

Is he sniffing the air? She pushed the thought aside.

"Well, as you can see, my sister-in-law is suffering from a severe headache today. I have come to help her out."

Anna had resumed her position on the cane chair with her feet propped on the stool and her hand over her forehead.

"Oh, I am greatly saddened to hear of your distress, Mrs. Russell."

I know he is sniffing the air.

"Yes, I had just brewed some … coffee for my sister-in-law to see if that might calm her pain." Betsy swallowed with difficulty.

Anna pulled the quilt across her belly even higher.

"I see." Deacon Adams' eyes narrowed.

Betsy spoke up quickly. "Might you join us," she smiled her most polite grin, "and take a cup of coffee as well?" Betsy tried to keep her voice steady, but her heart was in her throat.

"Unfortunately, Miss Russell, I must decline. Far be it from me to cause further discomfort for Mrs. Russell during such a time. I pray that you recover forthwith, Mrs. Russell. Good day." He tipped his tricorne at the ladies, winked at Betsy, and let himself out.

Betsy held her breath as she watched him walk down the puddle-filled road. Turning toward her sister-in-law, Betsy burst out laughing. Anna managed a slight smile while holding her head.

Picking up the pewter pot, Betsy held it with trembling hands. "Some coffee, Anna?"

 **5**

Tomorrow is Sabbath again. Lord, forgive me, but 'tis becoming a painful trial indeed, listening to the patriot rhetoric from the pulpit. It fills my heart with despair. Lord help us! And please—spare me from the "beautiful" Polly Cutter who looks at me as if I were a toad. She is the meanest girl in Menotomy. But I wish I had her beauty.

~ Diary of Betsy Russell, 11 March 1775

MARCH 1775

"Be not ye afraid of them; remember the Lord which is great and terrible, and fight for your brethren, your sons, and your daughters, your wives and your houses."

Betsy shuddered as Reverend Cooke bellowed from the pulpit. Quoting from the Old Testament book of Nehemiah, he brought the present plight of Menotomy Village into a far too personal comparison with the Jews of old battling their enemies.

Thoughts of her parents and Noah as they melted down the pewter plates after breakfast this morning filled her mind with terror. Their very utensils being turned into musket balls! She had never witnessed such a sight before.

She would never forget the furrowed worry on her parents' brows as they concentrated on pouring the molten metal into the molds to make the balls—shots that might be used not to kill a deer or bear, but a human. Perhaps a king's soldier? Surely this could not happen in her village.

Dear Lord, please do not allow this to occur.

Fighting the nausea that welled in her stomach, she dared to glance at her father. His lips were pressed firmly together, and the occasional twitch in his jaw surprised her. She had never seen his face this grave.

Forcing herself to turn away, she glanced at young Josiah sitting next to her. He scrawled chalk letters on a slate board, seemingly oblivious of the frightening words from the pulpit. *I wish I were only seven years old. Too young to understand what is happening.*

But even at eighteen, Betsy still did not understand all that occurred in Massachusetts. She knew that taxation was at the forefront of the tension between England and the colonies. But what had happened in the last four years was beyond disturbing.

Ever since word that a massacre of ordinary Boston citizens by British troops had reached Menotomy in 1770, a seed of worry had taken root in Betsy's heart. Were they safe a mere six miles from Boston?

Betsy heard her father say that King George had sent thousands of troops to Boston. He said the Committee of Safety had set up units of Minutemen in every town and village in the colony. Their presence in Menotomy increased daily.

What does all this mean?

The Reverend's voice rose to a crescendo, drawing her thoughts back to the front of the meetinghouse.

"And now, brethren, the case we have been considering in Nehemiah is recorded for our instruction. It is with the deepest regret that we in any degree apply these to ourselves in the present gloomy day. The adversaries of Judah were foreigners, they were pagans. These similar, horrible attempts now—right here in Massachusetts—constrain us to say that it is Britons who are our adversaries! That Englishmen thirst for our blood! That our most gracious, sovereign George III declares us rebels!

"Our adversaries, we may conclude, have long—by repeated insults—endeavored to provoke us to some act that might be represented as rebellious. But disappointment appears only to have enhanced their rage, and the vengeance long since cursed by one born among us is now pointed at our breasts.

"There, at present, appears no other choice left us but either sit down tamely and surrender our lives and properties, our wives and children, our religion and consciences to the arbitrary will of others, or, trusting in God, to stand up in our own defense."

Betsy wiped damp palms on her gown, grateful the moisture would not leave an imprint of her anxiety on the woolen material.

The congregation stood for the final prayer and hymn, and Betsy managed to hit a few notes on key. The rest of the melody came out thick with grief. As the assembly exited, she rested her hand on Josiah's shoulder in a gentle, motherly manner, prodding him toward the meetinghouse door. To her surprise, he did not pull away but leaned closer toward her.

Perhaps Josiah understands more than I thought.

She noticed that Reverend Cooke was not bidding his usual farewell to the parishioners from the doorway. Instead, he stayed at the front of the meetinghouse, making himself available to the congregation. Several patriots listened to his impassioned voice as they gathered around him near the pulpit. Betsy overheard the words "this trying situation" before leaving the wooden building.

A blast of chilled air whipped her bonnet's ribbons across her cheek. The frigid wind stung her face as she looked up at the looming clouds.

"Looks like a blizzard comin'." Her father's voice interrupted her family's silence. "Best get on home, eat quickly, then gather the stock."

All were somber as they trudged down Concord Road toward home. The driving wind, increasing during the half-mile journey, thrust the women's long skirts sideways. Betsy felt the cold draft all the way up her bare legs.

I wish I had put on a few more petticoats.

She clenched her skirts tightly with one hand while using her other hand to help Josiah move forward against the battering, wintry force.

Arriving at the house, Betsy's father appeared out of breath. His ruddy face was already chapped. "Betsy, Noah—we must gather the stock before we eat."

Elizabeth and Josiah went inside while Betsy and Noah followed their father toward the huge meadow behind their house. Snow started to fall, and Betsy closed her mouth against the frigid particles. Covering her nose against the stinging cold, Betsy shouted above the wind. "Father, where are the cows?"

"They may have gone near the woods, or perhaps they're in the orchard. Don't want them calvin' in the snow."

With the driving wind, it took twice as long to traverse the acres in search of the animals. Since the apple orchard was closest, they headed there first. Betsy noticed that the bare branches had not started to bud.

At least that is one blessing. Snow would kill them for certain.

They heard a distant bellowing and followed the sound. There, next to one large apple tree, stood two of the cows, bellies swollen with their unborn calves.

"Well, there's two. Still need to find Old Tess. She's the closest to givin' birth."

Jason pointed at the two cows in the orchard. "You two grab their ropes and draw them toward the barn. I'll go look for Tess."

As Betsy and Noah grasped the cold ropes, Betsy's bare hands instantly went numb.

Lord, help me not drop this rope.

The animals were in no hurry to leave the partial shelter of the orchard and resisted the siblings' efforts to take them away. Noah and Betsy pulled with enough force that the reluctant bovines followed them to shelter, several hundred feet from the orchard. By the time they arrived at the relative warmth of the birthing barn, Betsy was out of breath and her nose ran freely. While gasping for air, she saw Noah wipe off his nose with his chapped, bare hand. "How do you fare?" she asked him.

"Well enough, Betsy. I can handle a man's work." Looking at his sister, he put one hand on his hip while holding the cow's rope with the other. "I should be askin' how *you're* farin'. You're a female, after all."

She made a face at her little brother. "Aye, and quite a capable one, I might add, *little* brother!" She scooped a clump of straw from the floor and threw it at him. She laughed, then remembered their instructions. "Let us settle the cows with fresh hay and straw."

They were silent for several moments while getting water buckets set up in each stall. Pumpkin the cat had followed them into the birthing barn and found a pile of thick straw to nestle in. The cold air had already frozen the surface of the water in the bucket, and it took a large stick to break through the solid layer so the cows could drink. The breath from the huge bovines billowed in puffs of vapor. Betsy and Noah leaned against the thick oak posts supporting the barn and watched them.

"Soon we shall have new calves." Betsy allowed herself a small grin at the prospect.

"Soon we shall have a war." Noah's words startled her.

"Aye." Silence ensued. "Are you frightened, Noah?"

"Aye." Noah seemed to lean closer to the wooden post. "Even though I can hold a musket, I'm not that good yet. No match for a king's soldier." He pushed his long hair off his shoulder. His eyes betrayed his concern.

"You need not fight with the men, Noah. You're only twelve."

"Aye—not a boy and not a man. What good am I?" She noticed his eyes glisten in the light coming through a knothole.

Resting her hand on his shoulder, Betsy gave him a gentle squeeze with her reddened fingers. "I need you, Noah. We all do. Whether you carry a musket or help us on the farm, we all need you."

"I wish I could do more."

"Aye. I think we all do."

The door swung on its leather hinges and their father arrived hauling a reluctant cow in obvious distress. "Tess is near birthin'. Lay a bundle of straw in the south corner."

Betsy and Noah hurried to grab armloads of straw and piled them as high as they could. Tess lay down on the mass of dried grass and breathed erratically.

"Glad I found her in time." Father rubbed his hands together and breathed onto his reddened fingers. "Noah, go pump more water into a bucket for her."

The boy found an empty bucket in a far corner, pulled his wool collar higher on his neck, and put his head downward as he went outside.

The sound of the wind ebbed slightly when the portal was closed.

Betsy and her father silently watched the cow lying on the hay. Small hooves protruded from the back end of the mother.

"It won't be long now." Father's face appeared more relaxed than it had earlier at the meetinghouse. A glint of joy shone in his eyes as he watched the small nose and mouth of the new calf slowly appear. A stream of water trickled out, and he grinned.

"Keep goin', Tess. You can do 'er."

In a matter of moments, a large, brown calf emerged from the mother cow. The female offspring lay on the fresh straw for a few minutes while Tess licked the blood and slippery covering from her calf. The newborn heifer's spindly legs wobbled as she struggled to stand. Once upright, she nursed at the mother's swollen udder.

"A fine calf, Tess. You've done well." Father grew more sober. "This might be her last one. She might not be with us much longer."

"She might have more calves, Father. She is not so old." Betsy reached out and touched his arm. He surprised her by grabbing her hand and holding it.

"Betsy." His mouth twisted with unexpected emotion. "You must promise me that no matter what happens, you'll stay with your mother—and Noah and Josiah. Stay with them and watch out for them. Do all you can to hide. No matter what happens. Do you understand?"

Betsy's heart lurched at the earnestness in his voice. Fighting back tears, she swallowed with difficulty. "Aye, Father. I understand."

"Do ya, lass?" His intent gaze captured her attention. "'Tis not just our lives at risk in these dangerous times, but our very future as Americans. We have much to lose if the men do not fight—our freedoms, our lands. But we have even more to lose if there are none of our children left to carry on."

He rested his hand gently on her shoulder. "I count on you the most, Betsy. You may someday find yerself tremblin' with fear, lass, but trust in the Lord. Do all you can to protect the family. You are the hope for our future."

Her father swept his only daughter against his chest. Betsy could not recall him holding her so tightly before, and it sent fear coursing through her.

Father is frightened as well!

She clung to him, afraid to ever let go.

6

The last of the calves has been born, and all are growing well. Such a joy to have new life when we seem surrounded by the fear of death. And soon Anna will bring more new life to the family. Dare I hope for a future where our lives, both young and old, are safe?

~ Diary of Betsy Russell, 5 April 1775

APRIL 6, 1775

Betsy's chest tightened at her father's announcement: The men of Menotomy were called to the meetinghouse.

"Pray, why? 'Tis a day to plow fields, not listen to sermons." Without thinking, she gripped the sleeve of his work coat. Betsy felt the tension in his muscles, even through the layer of wool.

His eyes met hers, filled with resignation and certainty. He squeezed her hand before he removed her clenched fingers from his sleeve. "Stay here and help your mother, Betsy." Turning toward his twelve-year-old son, he gestured toward the door. "Come with me, Noah."

Betsy's head swam with confusion and anger.

My little brother gets to go, yet not I?

Struggling to control her tongue, she glanced with pleading eyes at her mother.

Without Betsy needing to say a word, her mother mouthed her answer. "No" was visibly, yet silently, spoken by her parent.

Betsy stared after her father and brother as they plodded down the steps on the east side of the house. As she watched them trudge toward the road, she bit her lip. On a morning filled with sunshine, her spirits lacked the brightness of the day. She saw others—Seth Stone, Thomas Cutter, Mathew Cox—all dressed for fieldwork yet carrying their muskets. They walked with purpose toward the meetinghouse, heads upright and alert. It looked to Betsy like they were already marching off to war.

Turning toward her mother, who was stirring the soup, Betsy struggled to voice her question. "Mother, why must Father go to this meeting? He is not one of the Minutemen." She gulped back the tears that threatened to erupt.

Elizabeth looked up from the hearth, and Betsy saw moisture in her mother's eyes. She doubted it was from the smoke in the fireplace.

"Your Father is a leader in this community. You may forget he was Selectman and Precinct Assessor before the plowing accident." Elizabeth turned back to the kettle and slowly stirred, her voice tremulous. "He would like to be amongst the Minutemen as one of them. His heart is a provincial soldier even though his body cannot conform. The rest of the village knows this, and they respect him."

Betsy stood for several moments without speaking. It had never occurred to her how the townspeople saw her crippled parent. She suddenly feared that she was losing Jason Russell, this man she had long loved as her devoted father. He was no longer just her parent and head of their home, but the leader in a cause larger and greater than their family. A man Menotomy Village looked upon as a head of the town. Shivering, she forced herself to move her limbs and continue cleaning the tableboard.

Josiah ran in with his wooden toy soldiers, but Elizabeth grabbed his shirt and stopped him. "Put the toys away, young lad. Time for reading."

A groan erupted from Josiah, but one look at his grandmother's face silenced any protest. He returned the wooden soldiers to his toy box upstairs and reappeared with his Bible and *Aesop's Fables*.

The boy sat on a brown-painted chair by the window, next to his grandmother. Betsy watched her mother reverently open the weathered pages of the Holy Scriptures and help Josiah sound out the words in the book of Genesis.

Trying not to disturb them, Betsy discreetly grabbed her shawl from the wall hook and attempted to slip out the front door, unnoticed.

Her mother's voice halted her. "Where are you going, daughter?"

"I thought I would check on Anna, since Thomas is likely at the meeting, as well." Betsy's answer seemed to satisfy her mother, because she resumed the reading lesson.

On her way to the meetinghouse, Betsy wrestled with her conscience. *Please forgive me, Lord.*

As if to somehow turn her lie into truth, she considered stopping by to see Anna after she listened to Reverend Cooke.

Betsy might not be invited to the gathering at the meetinghouse, but she determined to listen to the proceedings—what was left of their discussion, anyway. She wondered how much had transpired before she got there. She quickened her pace as she walked the hundred rods to the community house, which was across the street from her brother Thomas' store.

She did not need to get close to the building to hear the bellowing voice of Reverend Samuel Cooke reverberate off the sounding board within. His deep voice easily reached her anxious ears outside.

Creeping closer, she found most of the windows open, allowing the warm spring air into the room. She could not look directly inside without being noticed. However, she heard enough loud grunts of affirmation from the crowd within to know the gathering bulged with patriotic fervor.

"While our enemies are opening their mouths wide against us by way of reproach, gaping for our possessions and our persons to be their slaves, let us pour out our hearts before God, for God is a refuge for us! Though the Royal ear appears fast closed against the voice of our calamities, the eyes of the Lord are upon the ways of men, and His ears are open to their cries."

Betsy's heart pounded. She shook her head to stop the ringing in her ears as she strained to hear every word that thundered from Reverend Cooke.

"If we are terrified into a submission, the other colonies will make the best terms they are able and leave us and our posterity to groan in chains of bondage. Our brethren in arms will duly consider this and set a leading example of undaunted fortitude. Let us all carefully study peace, unity, and good order among ourselves and avoid all just occasion of offence to any person. Let none, under any provocations, thirst for blood, but let your breasts strongly beat for the liberty of your country!"

At this fervent statement, the entire meetinghouse exploded with pounding hands against wooden pews and loud shouts of "Hear, hear!"

Her throat completely void of moisture, Betsy cowered underneath the window, then scurried away from the building. She breathed so fast that her head and hands tingled. Regardless, she kept running as if her feet were not under control of her conscious thoughts. She ran, hoping that the farther she got from the meetinghouse, the better she could keep the drums of war at bay.

Deep within, she knew that escape was a hopeless dream.

7

I cannot sleep. My mind races with thinking of the countenances in Menotomy, so filled with resignation. They speak without using words. Never has silence screamed so loudly. I cover my own ears with my hands but 'tis useless. For the voices shout inside my own mind telling me the same terrifying declaration. War is at hand.

~ Diary of Betsy Russell, 14 April 1775

APRIL 15, 1775

Her father's prayer over the noontime meal was interrupted by heavy pounding at the front door. The fiery grip on Betsy's stomach reignited, a sensation all too familiar with the increasing tensions.

She watched her father struggle from his chair, musket in hand. He opened the door to a frantic Solomon Bowman, lieutenant of the Menotomy Minutemen.

"Have you heard the news?" Solomon's dirt-covered face was smeared with sweat and worry.

"Nay, Solomon. What now?"

"One of them British spies was in Concord all last week, posing as a gunsmith. He got Major Buttrick on his good side and Buttrick—fool that he was—believed he could trust the man. Shot off his big mouth to the bloody-back about where the supplies and arms were kept. Now the blaggart's gone back to Boston, most likely to inform General Gage. We'll be seein' a few visitors marching now, for certain."

Betsy watched her father clench and release his jaw before speaking. "You know for a fact? He was a spy?"

"One of Buttrick's men followed him after he left. He said he'd get his tools for fixin' muskets. Instead of going to Pownall Burough like he said, he headed straight to Boston. Right to Governor Hutchinson's butchers." Solomon's face glowed bright red as he spat out his words.

Betsy's father stared at the floor while one hand gripped the door and the other rested on his musket as a crutch. He seemed to recover himself. "Come in for some cider, Solomon."

"Nay, Jason, thanks all the same. Got to spread the word." He tipped his hat, and Betsy watched him hurry to untether his brown mare from the gatepost.

Betsy's father slowly closed their door, and its creaking hinge pierced the silence in the room. At the sound, Betsy's mother glanced up with widened eyes. Father stared blankly for a long moment before turning back to his family.

"Let's finish our prayer. And eat. Sabbath begins at dusk."

Her father slowly sat down and bowed his head. The words of his prayer were so mumbled, Betsy could not hear them. Yet, she saw his hand shake as he held her mother's. Tears dripped onto his lap. They reminded her of the blood that pulsed from the wound of young Mrs. Fessenden years before. Betsy shuddered uncontrollably.

8

'Tis a beautiful spring evening. Too beautiful for war.

~ Diary of Betsy Russell, 18 April 1775

APRIL 19, 1775
1:00 AM

The thundering sound in her head grew louder. Clomp, clomp, splash. More clomping.

Am I dreaming?

Betsy sat up in bed, only half awake. She stared at the window she'd propped open with a stick and shook her head while trying to make sense of the sound.

A horseman? In the middle of the night? What time is it?

She covered her mouth to stifle a yawn. When she heard an earnest voice yelling from the road, she jumped. "The regulars are coming! To arms! The regulars are coming!"

Clutching her quilt to her chin, Betsy was instantly wide-awake. From the room below, she heard her father's voice as he shouted to the rider, who must have paused in front of their house.

"What say you, man?" Her father's voice sounded garbled with sleep.

Heart racing, Betsy threw off the quilt and leaped from her bed. Bending down at the window to get a better view of the rider and horse in the bright moonlight, Betsy noticed the mount was lathered in sweat and breathed heavily. The rider removed his hat and wiped his face while speaking with her father.

"Gage's troops are on their way to Concord. Make ready. Gather the Minutemen and make your stand by daybreak. To arms!" With that, the rider jolted his steed with a kick and continued his journey. His fading voice could be heard in the distance. "To arms! The regulars are coming!"

Betsy clutched the windowsill with trembling hands. Her legs shook, and she lowered herself to the cold, wooden floor against her will. Her parents' voices murmured in the room below. Bending her knees, she hugged them tightly and buried her face in the linen material covering her thighs.

Grateful that Noah and Josiah were in the south bedroom, away from the road, she prayed they would not awaken. *Time enough for terror after a night's rest*, she reasoned amidst the frantic fear racing through her mind. *Where is my knife? I must dress. Where are my shoes? Does one need to wear stays if she is going to war? Such a ridiculous thought, Betsy Russell.*

The sound of steps made her jump and clutch her linen shift at her breast.

"'Tis I, Betsy."

"Father!"

She pushed herself off the floor and ran into his arms. For a moment, no words were spoken. Pulling her away from his tender grip, he looked into her eyes.

"Go back to bed for now, lass. There is naught to occur this night. We must face them on the morrow. They march to Concord, and we will let them pass through Menotomy tonight. We can do naught 'til daylight."

"But Father—"

"Do not wake the lads." He held up his finger to his lips. "The army will likely be hell-bent on their goal. They will not stop at every house along the road. At sunrise, we shall make plans to keep you all safe— when the troops journey back to Boston. For now, back to bed, lass."

Back to bed? Rest? When Gage's troops are coming?

As if reading her mind, her father walked her back to her four-poster bed. "I'll stand guard at the window, in the dark and with my firelock, Betsy." There was much she wanted to say—to ask—but the words lodged in her constricted throat. Her father covered her shivering frame with the quilt made years ago by her mother. "Rest now." It was a command but spoken with gentleness and love.

She managed two words. "I shall."

Patting her on the head, he limped away and left the room. She heard him check on the sleeping boys across the hall before slowly descending the narrow, curved stairway with the uneven steps. His careful footsteps clomped back to the room below. As she lay trembling under the covers, Betsy heard mumbled whispers between her parents.

Clutching the edges of her soft quilt, she fought back tears that welled behind her eyelids. *How am I supposed to rest? An entire army heads our way!* As she turned onto her side, the tears overflowed and rolled onto her pillow. She sniffed softly, as she did not wish her parents to hear her crying. *Lord, help me not to cry. Help me rest—as Father wishes.*

2:00 AM

It seemed only a few moments before an unfamiliar sound thrust her upright once again. Her heart took on a new beat as the strange and rapid thumping sound grew louder. It stirred her blood with a chill that sent its icy prickle from her feet all the way to her neck.

Soon, the candleholder on her small table danced, reverberating to the increased pounding on the road. She clutched the unlit lamp, lest it fall to the floor, placing it on the soft mound of her bedding to keep it steady.

Betsy fought the grip of nausea in her belly and forced her stiffened legs from under the covers. Stepping gingerly and with an unsteady gait, she crouched down and made her way to the open window. Standing to the side so she could not be seen, she peered carefully around the edge of the window jamb. The scene below sent ripples of terror through her body and mind. It was unlike anything Betsy had ever imagined in the deepest recesses of her fears.

Pounding the muddy road right next to their stone wall, soldiers of the king's army—splendid and frightening in their royal red uniforms—trudged in unison, four abreast. Their faces were stoic and determined in the moonlight, and their beaver hats made them look as tall as Goliath. The most frightening image, however, was the silvery row of gleaming bayonets. Situated in perfect array on the shoulders of the regulars marching in expert time, the flowing wave of exposed steel weapons rippled like a smooth river in the moonlight. It was both beautiful and terrifying.

Betsy's breathing came in gasps that she tried to smother with her hand. Her heart took on an irregular beat that refused to keep time with the king's army. Just as her knees began to weaken and give way, she jolted back to alertness when Josiah burst into her bedchamber.

"Aunt Betsy! I'm frightened." His voice was loud and likely audible through the open window—even above the pounding of the boots.

Betsy lunged toward the boy and grabbed him close to her while covering his mouth. She pulled him back against the wall and gripped him with a fervor that was sure to increase his fear.

Had they heard him? Betsy closed her eyes *tightly. Dear Lord, help us!*

Desperately wanting to keep her eyes shut, she forced her lids open while still covering Josiah's mouth. Carefully peering around the edge of the window frame, she panicked when she saw two lobsterbacks had fallen out of the line. They talked and pointed at her window. Terror seized her, but she knew she must remain strong for Josiah.

Lord, help us. Please, make them go on their way.

Josiah clung to her without making a sound, so she slowly removed her hand from his mouth. She bent down slightly and mouthed near his face, "Not a sound."

He nodded, his eyes wide and filled with fear. He clung to her, apparently forgetting he was too old to need her comfort.

She stroked his soft hair away from his face and silently prayed for protection.

Just then, the meetinghouse bell pealed, calling the town "to arms." Betsy's dry throat rebelled against her efforts to swallow. She envisioned falling over from fright and was grateful that Josiah was there. Despite his frailty, he unwittingly stood as a bulwark of strength to keep her upright.

After a few moments of sheer terror, Betsy dared to risk a quick glance out the window again. The two soldiers were gone. The entire brigade was marching faster toward the west—and the provincial stores of weapons in Concord.

Dear God, please. Don't let them steal our weapons.

Josiah began to whimper and Betsy held the boy closer. They waited, pressed against the wall and away from the window, for what seemed like hours. Betsy lost all track of time. *How many troops went by? Hundreds? Thousands?* Her head spun and, despite the cool night air, sweat dripped down her face.

How will the Minutemen in Concord fight against so many? We are so few, and they have so many weapons.

When the king's army had finally passed Menotomy—away from Betsy's home—she weakly guided Josiah toward her bed. They both fell onto the edge of her mattress, and Josiah burst into tears. "I want my Mother! Where is Father?"

Betsy wrapped her arm around his shoulders and stroked the side of his head. She tried her best to comfort him. "Your mother and father are in New Hampshire, but they'll be here soon." She hoped that was so—for Josiah's sake.

Of course he wants his parents. I wish I could curl up in my own mother's lap right now—like when I was small. Mother and Father would make everything all right, everything safe. How she wished they could do so tonight.

9

I will say of the Lord, He is my refuge and my fortress: my God;
in Him will I trust ... Thou shalt not be afraid for the terror by night;
nor for the arrow that flieth by day.

Psalm 91:2, 5

APRIL 19, 1775
5:00 AM

The sun had not yet risen when Betsy and her mother heard voices coming toward their house. None of the Russell family had slept since the appearance of the regulars marching through the village. None, save Noah, who reposed in the bedroom upstairs.

I wish I were so unaware of this terrible day.

Betsy held Josiah on her lap as the boy occasionally closed his eyes. Every small sound startled the child awake. Sitting by the hearth for warmth, Betsy longed for the days when Josiah would snuggle on her lap in comfort rather than distress. She continued to stroke his head, as much for solace of her own fears as the boy's. A knock at the door and earnest shouts for "Jason Russell!" caused her mother to stop stirring the gruel over the hearth and hurry to answer.

"Mr. Bowman." Mother did not seem surprised to see the lieutenant of the militia.

He tipped his hat politely, but his face was drawn in concern. "Where be your consort, Mrs. Russell?"

Betsy saw her mother visibly swallow. Her voice was small. "He is in the barn, oiling his musket."

Father appeared at the back door carrying his gun. "Solomon. What news have ye?"

46

Rage fired in Solomon's face. "Those bloody-backs! One of them left ranks on the road, askin' for water when I opened my door. 'What are you out at this time of night for?' I asked him. Must've scared the butcher back to his company." He glanced quickly around the room at Elizabeth and Betsy. "Beggin' your pardon, ladies."

Her mother nodded and returned to the hearth. Betsy had never seen her so pale and walk with such weariness.

Solomon turned toward Betsy's father. "Much happened in the hours of darkness, Jason. You know the Committee of Safety met at the Black Horse Tavern last night. Well, three of them stayed the night, living so far away and all. When them troops hauled through town, they sent out several regulars to search the place. The three members barely escaped outside in the cold darkness, forced to hide in the stubble in the cornfield so they wouldn't be seen. Barely escaped with their underclothes on their backs. Old Colonel Lee's not doin' so well this morning, I hear."

Betsy's tired eyes widened.

The king's troops were here? They searched the tavern?

She already felt sick to her stomach, but with this news she squeezed her eyes shut momentarily, as if she could block out the reality of their situation.

"Others had soldiers stop by as well. Tuft's barn was searched; at least his favorite horse was loaned out yesterday. Kept her out of them lobsterbacks' hands." He shook his head, then looked inquisitively at Jason. "Anyone stop here?"

Betsy's father lifted his eyes to meet Solomon's. "Nay. None came to our door."

Thank you, Heavenly Father!

"Well, then, I'll be off. The Minutemen will meet on the green by daybreak." He paused. "Most of the men are taking their wives and young ones up the hill to the Prentiss house. You and your family will be safe there. Look sharp. Someone saw riders in red coats heading back toward Boston. Likely they'll be bringing reinforcements through here." Solomon directed an intense gaze. "Look sharp, Jason. Guard yer family."

Even by the dim light of the hearth, Betsy could see her father's face fill with defeat. After a moment, he spoke.

"Aye, Solomon. I'll take my family to the Prentiss.'"

"Good. We need marksmen like yourself to watch out for our loved ones. God be with you, Jason."

He put his hand on Solomon's shoulder. "Godspeed, Solomon. Kill a few bloody-backs for me."

The men stood there silently for a moment before Solomon tipped his hat to the group.

"Good day, Jason. Mrs. Russell. Miss Russell. Lad."

Her father stood at the open door, gripping his musket tightly. After a moment, he closed the door and turned back toward his wife. "Best get the family fed soon, Elizabeth." He looked around the room. "Where be Noah?"

NOON

"Jason, we must needs be off to the Prentiss house. The rest of the town has fled to safety." Although her mother tried to hide the fear in her voice, Betsy could hear it plainly.

Her father finished making another musket ball from the pewter plate he had just melted down. It was the last of the batch of bullets. As he popped open the round mold, he let the ball cool a moment before clipping off the sprue—the metal tag that formed when the molten pewter was poured. He held the round ball up for inspection and looked at it through squinted eyes.

"Aye, Elizabeth." He put the pile of newly-made bullets into his deerskin sack. "Just needed to be sure we had enough."

There could never be enough musket balls to protect us from Gage's troops.

Betsy held her tongue and kept her frightened musings to herself.

Her mother had packed their valuables to take with them. Their pewter tankards and the rest of their plates were tied in a sack and hidden in the bottom of the well in case the enemy ransacked their home. When Betsy had watched her father lower the sack into the deep pit, she felt like it was the burial of her once-secure past. She shivered even as she thought of it now.

Gathering her own basket of personal items—comb, clothing, sewing needles, lavender water—Betsy double-checked her pocket as she had done a dozen times this day. The padded sewing pouch and her knife remained intact.

As her family left their home, Betsy watched one somber-faced person after another walk past. The bleakest countenance belonged to Noah, who had berated himself all morning for sleeping through the entire enemy march through Menotomy. She could not count the number of times she had heard him moan, "Pray, why did you not awaken me?"

After exiting the house with one hand resting on Josiah's shoulder, Betsy turned to look for her father. All she could see was the back of his head, his long, grey hair pulled back with a ribbon, fluttering in the gentle breeze. His queue waved like a flag of remembrance that honored the end of their peaceful, pastoral existence. It was a painful realization for Betsy that their lives would never be the same.

She stood motionless until her mother's voice broke the solemnity of the moment. "Jason! We must hasten!"

Betsy's father appeared reluctant to leave, but he turned to accompany his family up the hill to their refuge.

Old man Whittemore came waddling down Concord Road armed with his musket, his sword from the last war, and a pistol.

"Samuel? What be your business? You're one of the exempts. Take shelter." Betsy's father faced the old man, concern etched on his face.

"That's what me wife said. I told her I was goin' uptown. Had some business to attend to. She clucked her head and headed for the Mystic."

Her father's eyes narrowed. "Samuel, you should take refuge with your wife and family."

The old man brandished his sword in the air. "I've lived eighty long years, Jason Russell. If my weapons draw blood from even one bloody-back, I'll consider I've been on God's earth long enough."

Betsy watched her father exhale in defeat. It seemed there was no reasoning with Samuel Whittemore.

The family walked several rods west before climbing up the hill toward the Prentiss home. The silence in the town was unnerving. There was no sign of the Minutemen anywhere. They likely faced the king's army in Concord at this very moment. Betsy tried not to envision the terror of that battle. She thought of her brother Thomas among them and squeezed her lips to keep the sobs from bursting forth.

All the women and children had escaped to their hideaways. Menotomy felt like a graveyard with spirits of the dead hovering close-by. She shuddered as she quickened her pace.

Looking across the hill, she noticed an orchard of peach trees in early bloom. The life in the trees was a stark contrast to her feelings of impending doom.

Josiah stopped in his tracks and whipped around toward the house. "Pumpkin! What about Pumpkin?"

Betsy squatted down and put a hand on his shoulder. "Cats know exactly where to hide, Josiah. She will out-fox those soldiers—never fear."

He seemed satisfied, and the silent group proceeded to the Prentiss home.

Her father, who was at the head of their pilgrimage to safety, stopped so abruptly that Noah ran into his back.

He turned around and handed his satchel of clothing to the twelve-year-old. "Noah, carry this." Their father visibly swallowed, but then he set his jaw in determination. "I am going back."

Betsy saw her mother start to sway, so she grabbed her arm.

"Jason?" Her mother's voice quivered.

He tenderly took his wife's other arm and caressed her face, now covered with rivulets of tears. He stood in silence, staring longingly at his wife, then tenderly at his children and grandson. Finally, he spoke.

"An Englishman's home is his castle."

The shocked moment of silence that followed was finally broken by young Josiah. "But, Grandsire." His mouth trembled. "You do not have a moat like the king does to protect *his* castle."

Jason smiled and sniffed. "Lad, I shall depend on the living water of God to protect me." He hugged the boy.

I beg you, dear Lord, let Father change his mind!

Instead, he released his grandson and looked him in the eye. "You stay with Betsy and your grandmother. Aye?"

"Aye." Josiah's voice was barely discernible.

"Elizabeth." He held his wife close. "I must go."

Betsy's mother tried to answer, but she covered her trembling mouth.

He released her and turned to his son.

"Noah, you be the man of the family now, 'til I get back."

"Aye, Father." Noah stood as tall as he could, and Betsy noticed his legs sway a bit.

Jason stood in front of his only daughter. "Betsy." He kept his voice low. "Remember, lass, I'm counting on you to keep everyone safe." His eyes pierced like a sword right through to her soul.

"Aye, Father," she whispered. "I'll not forget." The words choked on her breath.

Without another word, he turned and limped down the hill. Mouths agape, the family stood watching.

Only Josiah waved slowly after him. "Godspeed, Grandsire. I shall see you forthwith."

A deep fear gripped Betsy's heart and melted through every pore. It was a most unsettling terror that filled her with an unspeakable grief.

Trying to shake away the foreboding, she grabbed Josiah's hand and looked at the family standing in silence.

"Let us be off then. We must hasten."

10

There shall no evil befall thee,
neither shall any plague come nigh thy dwelling.

Psalm 91:10

APRIL 19, 1775
1:00 PM

Those taking refuge at the Prentiss home—perhaps fifty women and children—filled the house to overflowing.

Youngsters who usually played outdoors on such a warm day were trapped inside as anxious mothers watched their every move. Older children stood in rapt attention wherever they could get a view of the activity beyond the house, occasionally exclaiming more bad news.

"More bloody-backs!" Noah gripped his musket tightly.

Betsy hurried to a window facing north toward Concord Road. From high on the hill, the line of redcoats stood more distant, yet just as terrifying as the night before. In the shimmering sunlight, bayonets glistened like a long necklace of jewels.

Such finery used to kill.

Anger surged through her veins as her heart raged against this army that had betrayed the colonists' trust. These uniformed soldiers were supposed to be warriors to defend them. Now they prepared to skewer them with weapons that far outmatched the farmers' muskets.

They have no heart.

Betsy bit back her thoughts, not daring to express them in the company of so many innocents seeking refuge.

"Noah, come away from the window!" Mother sat on a chair holding a sleeping Josiah, who had finally succumbed to last night's exhaustion. "They may see you."

Noah did not move. "Someone has to keep guard, Mother." He gripped his firelock with manly bravery.

Betsy stole a glance down the hill again. "What is happening, Noah?"

He shifted on his foot and stood taller. "They're sending reinforcements to Concord. Mr. Bowman said riders had returned to Boston last night—likely for more troops. And here they are." He pressed his lips together tightly and stared like a hawk at his prey through the glass panes.

Would Noah be so brave if the enemy were closer? She doubted it—yet his presence holding the musket was still a comfort.

"There goes the end of the detachment." Noah peered around. "Except that wagon load of supplies bringing up the rear."

Two young boys chasing each other nearly ran into Noah and his firearm. He grabbed one by the collar of his shirt. "Look sharp! No time for play!"

His stern tone made the boys pause and all the mothers stop their conversations. Noah had become one of the men in charge.

Anna sat next to her mother-in-law, wincing. She rubbed her huge belly and whimpered.

"Mrs. Russell, ye must head for the birthing room now." Mrs. Prentiss pushed her large form through the mass of children and cleared a path toward a small room in the back of the house, part of a lean-to that her husband had added years ago.

Betsy hurried to the pregnant woman's side. "Let me help you, Anna." She gently grasped her sister-in-law's arm and helped her stand. Anna leaned on Betsy and walked with difficulty through the narrow path cleared by Mrs. Prentiss.

Just then a round of musket fire from the road shattered the already tense atmosphere. Children and women screamed.

Betsy looked back at Noah, who had turned deathly pale. "Noah, what is it?"

Another boy looking through the window said, "They shot those men! And the horses!"

"What?" Betsy gasped and gripped her throat with one hand while holding Anna with the other. Anna cried. Mrs. Hanscomb, one of the midwives, took over escorting Anna while Betsy fumbled her way toward her younger brother.

She pushed past Noah and stared at the unbelievable sight. Some of the British regulars were lying still as stones on the road, some writhing in apparent pain.

Several British soldiers ran off through a field toward Spy Pond but were shot at by several of the elderly local men who had been exempted from joining the Minutemen.

"David Lamson." Betsy said the old man's name in disbelief as she watched him and the other veterans regroup and stare at the carnage. Reverend Cooke hurried over from the meetinghouse nearby, and they spoke at great length. Then, several of the men hauled the carcasses of the dead horses away from the road and others pulled the supply-laden British wagons down into a hollow just off the road.

Betsy realized she could barely breathe because she was squeezing her throat so tightly. She released her clenched fingers and forced herself to inhale. Down the hall, Anna moaned in the birthing room.

"Betsy!" Her mother's voice carried to her ringing ears. "I said you must go to Anna. Josiah is sound asleep in my arms."

As if waking from a bad dream, Betsy shook her head and forced her feet to move toward the birthing room. Children tumbled everywhere and women cried and talked wildly. She pushed through the chaos and focused on her destination. She kept envisioning the dead soldiers. No, it was the living ones in pain that stayed in her thoughts. Pain gripped her own stomach.

"Mrs. Prentiss. Where is the back door? I must use the privy."

The grey-haired woman looked at her and grabbed her arm. "Are you ill, my dear?"

"A little. I need to relieve myself."

Betsy stumbled outside and searched for the small building. After relieving herself, she left the small enclosure and leaned on the wooden frame. She covered her face with her clenched fingers, trying to block out the images of the writhing British soldiers.

It was a scream from the birthing room that drew Betsy's attention back from her own pain.

Dear Lord, I must help Anna. I must keep the family safe, as Father said. Please—Father in heaven—give me strength.

With great resolve, Betsy pushed herself away from the small building and forced her wooden legs to move toward the birthing room.

I must be strong. God, help me be strong.

4:00 PM

Anna's pains increased after hours of laborious effort. The midwife walked her around the small room as much as the young mother could tolerate, but Anna's deep discomfort made those frequent ventures fewer by the hour.

The noise level from the main room next door increased. The assistant midwife looked up when Anna's most recent pain had ebbed. "What is the ruckus out there now?" She seemed more annoyed than worried.

Anna looked worried.

"Let me see what it is. I'm certain 'tis naught." Betsy forced a smile toward Anna and patted her on the shoulder before hurrying away.

Frantic faces and rapid voices confronted Betsy the moment she entered the main room.

"I tell ya, 'tis God's truth! The slaves are conspirin' against us! Mrs. Perry's niece said that her negro has been lookin' at her all day like he's a-plottin' to join the bloody-backs! They've just been waitin' on this day, I tell ya!" Mrs. Smith nodded her head with the certainty of her words.

Her rapt audience of frightened women hugged their children closely. They seemed completely convinced that the slaves would use this attack on the village as an opportunity to free themselves from their white owners. Mrs. Henry visibly swallowed and added her opinion.

"I thought I saw my Nancy peering at me sideways-like. Never did see her do that afore! She must be plottin' something awful. I thought … I thought I saw her grabbing a kitchen knife from the table board. Maybe she's going to murder me when my back's to her!"

The women inhaled sharply with terror in their eyes. A pounding at the door was met with a few screams. One of the boys looked out at the front step. "It's Ishmael! Mr. Cutler's slave!"

Mrs. Henry screamed uncontrollably.

Betsy could stand no more. "Please! I am certain 'tis only rumor. I vow, you must calm yourselves!"

"Noah, get your musket ready to shoot!" Mrs. Smith directed Betsy's brother.

Betsy cringed with horror at the thought of Noah shooting Ishmael. She clenched her fists and pushed her way through the mass of crying children. "No! Noah, put that firelock away. Let me go to the door."

"Betsy, no!" This time it was her mother's voice filled with panic. "You do not know if these rumors may be true!"

Determined to stop this hysteria—not to mention the possible killing of the kindly Ishmael—Betsy forced her way to the door, pushing Noah's musket down toward the floor in case it went off accidentally. "Noah, step aside!"

A look of confusion crossed his face, but he obeyed his older sister. Taking in a deep breath, she opened the door to the frightened gasps of several of the women.

Ishmael stood there, eyes wide, gripping his felt hat, glancing around nervously.

"Are you going to kill us, Ishmael?" Betsy did not mince her words as she looked pointedly at the servant.

"Lord-a-massey, no ma'am." His eyes searched the room. "Is my missus here?"

Betsy's heart calmed. "Aye, Ishmael. Come inside where you can be safe."

"No where's safe, ma'am. Soldiers is everywhere."

Betsy thought the teenager was going to cry. "You're safe with us,

Ishmael." She patted his shoulder and looked pointedly at Mrs. Smith, who avoided Betsy's penetrating gaze.

"Well, he cannot sit with us in this main room." Mrs. Smith blotted her moist face with her kerchief.

Mrs. Prentiss stood tall and put both hands on her hips. "'Tis my house, Mrs. Smith, and I shall decide who sits in the main room and who does not. Perhaps ye would feel more comfortable in the attic."

Mrs. Smith huffed and looked away.

Betsy smirked, but anger surged through her veins. She had found the issue of slavery for the Negroes in their community in direct opposition to the colonists' voices declaring that all men should be free under God. Was not Ishmael a young man?

Thoughts of this dilemma brought to mind Katy, their own slave who had died a few years before. She had been a friend to Betsy, who mourned her death most piteously. Katy. How she wished her friend could be here with her now to tell her things would all end well. Fighting back tears, Betsy heard a loud cry from the birthing room.

Thoughts of rumors and slavery dissipated as she ran toward the birthing room, focusing now on her sister-in-law laboring to deliver her brother Thomas' firstborn.

In the small room at the back of the house, Betsy was horrified to see Anna so distressed. Covered with sweat, Anna wore only a thin linen shift; the material clung to the length of her body. The midwife rubbed Anna's back, which offered some relief, though Anna writhed nevertheless.

Betsy felt helpless. She looked at Anna's mother, who had now joined the group in the crowded room. "'Tis the very same distress I was in during my birthins."

Anna's mother tried to smile, but she looked more like she could start to cry.

The midwife directed Betsy. "Hold one of her hands, lass."

The midwife's helper threw the window open wider, but the weather was so unusually warm that this provided little relief. Sips of water and a few sips of wine were offered Anna, who swallowed them with difficulty as she grasped her swollen, firm belly. Groans emerged from Anna. "I feel sick." Her mother wiped a damp cloth on her daughter's forehead.

And then it started in the distance—musket fire.

At first there were just a few popping sounds. But then they moved closer. The pops turned into sharp bursts of ignited gunpowder propelling metal balls—both whistling and menacing. The number of reports grew into a cacophony of explosive terror. Then there came the horrible sound of a thunderous blast, followed by the wails of the wounded—perhaps the dying. Betsy had never before heard anything like this.

"What was that?" Betsy's voice barely emerged from her throat.

The midwife looked up toward the sound, losing focus on her patient for a moment. "'Tis cannons." Just as quickly, she refocused on Anna.

Betsy saw Anna's eyes widen. "Thomas! I want Thomas!" The young wife wailed pitifully.

"Yer husband is fine, Anna. Now think about his wee child. 'Tis time ye birthed this young one, aye?" The midwife coaxed her tenderly.

Anna sobbed. "Aye." Tears flowed into her mouth.

Betsy grabbed a kerchief from her pocket and dabbed Anna's tears. She prayed her own would not begin to fall as she held tightly to Anna's grip.

Betsy could not discern if the sweat on her palms was from her own fear or from the intensity of Anna's pain.

She trembled at the events occurring outside on the nearby road as well as in the birthing room. She intertwined her fingers with those of her sister-in-law so tightly that Anna's labor pains coursed through Betsy's arms.

Anna screamed as a contraction gripped her swollen belly. Betsy clung to her as if she could take away the pain by the pressure of her grip. But before the pain ebbed, another sonorous blast of cannon fire echoed from hundreds of rods down the hill. The concussion reverberated throughout the house, and the walls shuddered along with her nerves. Even the midwife, normally a pillar of calm, turned pale.

Betsy desperately fought back fearful tears.

Why did Father not come with us?

She remembered his comforting hand on her shoulder months ago, the night he first said he was meeting with the patriot committee. He smiled at her then. All was as it should be with the world. But that seemed so long ago.

Another round of explosives elicited uncontrollable shivering.

Where is he now when I need his reassuring presence? Dear Lord, protect him.

The women in the room jumped when an enormous volley of musket fire rattled from the direction of Concord Road. Betsy doubted the pain-filled screams she heard were only in her imagination.

Father in heaven, this cannot be happening. How did we get to this terrible place? Dear Lord, help us.

11

Demons from hell had taken over the village. The low-lying terrain acted as a sounding board for the barrage of screams and gunfire. In all her life, Betsy had never heard such gut-wrenching sounds.

Dear God, make it stop!

There were cries of pain and anger interspersed with more musket volleys and shouts of "Look sharp!" followed by pistol shots. Breaking glass. The occasional cannon shot followed by screams—always more screams.

With the sounds of pain and pandemonium from Concord Road as a backdrop, Anna's desperate labor increased. The distraught mother-to-be nearly took leave of her senses, shouting curses at the women in the room and biting the pillow behind her head. She wailed, but Betsy had no fear that the British soldiers in Menotomy Village would hear. Anna's cries were like a whimper in comparison to the sounds of battle.

A deep moan emanated from Anna, a low growl that sent shivers through Betsy's spine. The midwife gave a satisfied nod. "Get 'er up to the birthin' stool."

Betsy's eyes squinted in confusion, but she followed Mrs. Hanscomb's directions.

The women guided Anna to the specially designed wooden chair that had a narrow rim and large opening through which the infant could descend. Betsy was ordered to support one of Anna's arms while Anna's mother was directed to hold the other arm.

Whenever Anna started her deep groaning, Mrs. Hanscomb urged her, "Push. Mrs. Russell, push."

In the midst of the fray, both within the room and from down the street, Betsy's mind wandered.

It seems so odd to hear Anna called Mrs. Russell. Mrs. Russell is my mother.

Betsy's strange thoughts abruptly stopped when an especially long volley of gunfire forced her mind back to reality. She wished she could let her mind continue to wander. Her daydreams transported her to a safer time and place, far away from the terror. Far away from the pain and death. She longed for escape—even if only in her imagination.

But freedom from reality was impossible when the sounds of war pierced through her dreams.

She glanced around for a chamber pot in case her churning stomach let go.

I've not eaten for hours. Surely nothing will come of my retching.

Swallowing back the acidic taste, she forced herself to focus on encouraging Anna's efforts to deliver her baby. She saw Mrs. Hanscomb bend low in front of Anna's splayed legs. "He's a comin'." The midwife's voice mixed relief with terror.

The child.

In all the horror, Betsy had forgotten that new life would soon displace the death that surrounded them.

It took several more pushes for poor, brave Anna. Betsy stared in both admiration and sheer sympathy for her sister-in-law. Anna's hair was undone, her shift soaked from hours of sweating, her eyes wide with madness from the excruciating pain.

I shall never bear a child. I'm grateful Amos left Menotomy. I'm grateful he left me.

Just then, Mrs. Hanscomb shouted. "'Tis a lass!"

The midwife held up the quivering child covered with blood and a thick, white paste. The little one screamed with new life, just as the last cry was heard from Concord Road. In the distance, the final round of musket fire could be heard as the invading troops finally left the colonists' once-peaceful village.

The midwife directed Betsy and the others to help Anna back onto the bed.

Betsy's eyes widened in terror at the amount of blood she saw. As if Mrs. Hanscomb understood this was Betsy's first birthing, the midwife said quietly to her, "'Tis the way of a birthin', lass. Anna will be fine."

"Thank you."

The tenderness in Mrs. Hanscomb's voice brought Betsy to tears. Betsy ran to the chamber pot, no longer able to quell her nausea. The midwife's assistant held her shoulders as she heaved uncontrollably for several moments. When she stopped, there was little to show for her body's efforts.

She wished she could discharge thoughts of this day from her senses, but not even vomiting could dislodge the images and sounds of war. Nor the knowledge that her life would never be the same.

What happened in our town? Who was injured? She could barely swallow. *Who was dead?*

Betsy was not capable of digesting that information any more than she could digest physical food. She never wanted to eat again.

The room was strangely quiet, save for the suckling noises of the young baby as Anna nursed her. Betsy was astonished at the calm look on her sister-in-law's face.

No one spoke. It seemed as if no one knew what to say or do. Betsy glanced up as her mother entered. "The child is well?"

"Aye, Mrs. Russell. Yer new granddaughter's a fine lass."

Mother began to close the door, then paused. "Betsy, go stay with Josiah and Noah."

Her legs felt as limp as linen rags, but she forced herself to stand and do as her mother asked.

I will not think about Concord Road.

Walking out to the main room, she saw Josiah sitting by himself on a wooden chair. Most of the children were quiet. A few lay on the floor with their hands still covering their ears and heads. None of the women spoke as they held whimpering youngsters on their laps.

Reaching Josiah, she put her hand on his shoulder. "Josiah?" He did not look up. Picking him up with her shaking arms, she sat down and, with effort, pulled him onto her lap. He buried his face on her shoulder and cried softly.

"T'will be all right, Josiah." Her own words stunned her.

T'will be all right? No. T'will never be right again.

At this realization, she buried her own face against Josiah's soft, pale hair and wept a deep and sorrowful cry.

12

Yea, though I walk through the valley of the shadow of death, I will fear no evil: for thou art with me; thy rod and thy staff, they comfort me.

Psalm 23:4

APRIL 19, 1775
6:00 PM

Betsy nodded off in the straight-backed chair while holding a sleepy Josiah. His heavy weight buttressed her in an upright position. Though he appeared comfortable, it was anything but a peaceful slumber for Betsy.

Whenever her chin dropped, she imagined cannon fire. Echoes of the dreadful memory shuddered through her tense frame. Awakening to find it was only a nightmare held little comfort for Betsy. She knew the nightmare was real.

When the door of the Prentiss house burst open, her head jerked upward. Her brother Thomas stood there panting. Betsy barely recognized him. It wasn't just the disheveled clothing and sweat-covered face of her sibling. It was his eyes—so hollow and haunting—his expression both vacant and terrified.

"Thomas?"

"Where is Anna? Is she well?" His voice was scratchy and husky—nothing like his usual clear resonance.

"Aye." Dare she ask? "Thomas, pray tell, what happened?"

He did not answer her question. Instead, "Where is she?"

Betsy stiffened at his lack of response to her question but pointed to the back room where Anna had delivered the baby. Thomas half stumbled, half ran to find his wife.

Betsy set Josiah's feet on the floor, took his hand, and followed her brother to the birthing room. She got there in time to see Anna reach out to her husband.

"Thomas!" Anna burst into tears of relief.

He leaned over and held her tightly for several moments. Kissing her enthusiastically, he looked down at the small child in her arms and stroked the baby's cheek. Anna handed the infant to her husband and smiled.

Thomas tenderly took his squirming daughter into his large hands. For a moment, he smiled. But, his pleasure seemed to melt away as his lips quivered uncontrollably. Handing the baby back to her mother, Thomas leaned down and kissed his wife again. Then, he stood silently and captured his mother's attention with his eyes. Taking her hand, he drew her gently out of the room.

Betsy stared after them, then heard the back door close. No one spoke a word. Her knees started to shake, so she sat on the edge of the birthing bed. Josiah plopped down next to her.

Noah appeared, rubbing his eyes. "Did I see Thomas?" He yawned.

"Aye." Betsy's voice was little more than a whisper. A piercing, powerful scream interrupted the stillness, hitting Betsy like a physical blow. She could not exhale her sharp intake of air.

Josiah grabbed Betsy's arm. "Is that Grandmother?" His small lips quivered.

Consciously forcing the air out of her lungs, she grasped his hand and drew him up from the edge of the bed. Focused on reaching the back door of the Prentiss house, she dragged Josiah with her, then noticed Noah close by, practically stepping on her heels. She thrust the door open with fumbling hands. The three stopped when they saw her mother clinging in desperation to Thomas. He held her without speaking, his eyes staring off into the distance. Their mother cried inconsolably.

"Grandmother?" The tone in Josiah's voice melted Betsy's heart.

Hearing her grandson, the grandmother's wails diminished. She wiped the voluminous tears from her cheeks with one hand, clinging to

Thomas with the other. Betsy could see that her mother's legs trembled as Thomas supported her.

Elizabeth stood up straighter and sniffed. Taking a deep breath, she appeared to gather her strength.

Betsy did not wish to hear her mother speak. She focused on the long grass that swayed in the gentle spring breeze. Looking upward, she saw a few clouds passing through the mostly-blue skies. But, while she could direct her eyes elsewhere, she could not stop her ears from hearing the news she dreaded.

"Josiah, your Grandsire is in heaven."

Noah's face turned red and his features contorted. "No!" He turned and raced toward the nearby woods, his screams echoing through the trees.

"Noah!" Mother started to run after him.

"Let him go." Thomas gently held her arm. "He needs to be alone."

Josiah shook his head. "I do not understand. Grandsire is home. He told us so." Tears brimmed in his eyes.

Thomas walked toward his nephew. "He did go home, Josiah, just as he said. But the bloody-backs killed him." Tears rolled down Thomas' cheek as he stooped down to face the child at eye level.

"Killed him?" Josiah could say no more as Thomas grabbed him and held him close. Uncle and nephew clung to one another.

Betsy stood stock-still. She could not speak. She could barely breathe. She was not certain she wanted to breathe.

"Betsy?" Her mother approached her, eyes narrowed and filled with concern.

"Aye, Mother?" The words came with difficulty.

"Did you hear what Thomas said?" Her mother searched her face.

"Aye, Mother." Betsy's limbs stiffened but she could not feel them. All of her senses focused on a strange ringing in her ears.

As if shocked by a bolt of lightening, she ran toward their house as fast as her legs could carry her.

"Thomas, stop her!" She heard her mother's insistent voice in the distance.

Betsy could not have stopped if she wanted to.

I must see Father.

Racing as fast as she could, she nearly fell when Thomas overtook her. As he grabbed her arm, she loudly demanded, "Let me go!"

He held both of her arms fast. "Nay, Betsy, you must not go into the house."

"Why not?" She did not recognize her enraged voice.

Thomas pulled her close and held her, even though she hit him and yelled for him to release her.

After all of her meager strength ebbed, all she had the energy to do was weep.

Thomas continued holding her, stroking the hair that had come undone from her mobcap.

His trembling voice broke as he spoke. "Betsy, there are twelve dead men laid out in front of the hearth. You must not go inside."

"Twelve?" She pulled away from him, searching his eyes.

"Aye." He swallowed with difficulty.

"So ... so twelve men were killed in our town?"

Thomas looked down and avoided her intense gaze. "Nay, Betsy. Many more than twelve."

Betsy's heart lurched with a strange rhythm. "More? How many?"

"Dozens. I do not know the number, Betsy." His eyes were moist. "Please, do not go inside the house."

"But I must see Father! Please—"

"Betsy, nay. You must remember him as he was. It is no longer Father there. Just his earthly vessel."

Elizabeth caught up with them, pulling a crying Josiah along with her.

"Betsy." Her mother struggled to catch her breath. "Stay with Josiah. Thomas, take me to the house."

"But Mother—"

"*Now*, Thomas."

He released Betsy and wearily walked toward the Russell home, holding his mother's arm. There were just a few rods left before arriving at Concord Road.

Heading east toward their house, Betsy followed at a distance behind them, clinging to Josiah's hand. The seven-year-old strode beside her in silence.

Betsy heard wailing throughout the otherwise quiet street. Men she did not recognize carried bodies toward ox carts. Occasionally, screams of pain burst from the mouths of the wounded when they were lifted and carried to makeshift infirmaries. Most of the casualties, however, were silent. The pall of death hung over them.

Betsy tried not to look at anyone's faces. She did not wish to stare into the faces of the dead.

Ammi Cutter, who lived across the way, came running toward the Russell house. His eyes sunk into a face red and contorted.

"Hutchinson's butchers! They killed your father like he was a pig! Not enough they had to shoot him down, but they used their savagery to stab him over and again!" Mr. Cutter yelled with hysteria.

Betsy's voice choked in her throat. Covering Josiah's ears, she stared without speaking. Her heart raged at the man's words.

Butchers!

Thomas glared at their neighbor, his voice cutting through the man's outburst. He gripped Mr. Cutter's arm. "Nay, Mr. Cutter. Do not speak of this!"

Mr. Cutter turned away weeping and walked toward his home.

Normally Betsy would have pity on the old man, but her mind filled with hatred for the soldiers who had done this terrible thing. There would be no room in her heart for forgiveness or compassion today.

At the opening in the stone wall, Betsy noticed piles of wooden shingles strewn about. It looked like they had been stacked together as some sort of defense then pushed aside. Thrown aside. She shivered uncontrollably as they approached the front stoop.

Thomas stopped walking and turned to Betsy and Josiah. "You both wait here."

Betsy had no inner reserve of strength to face what lay within the walls of her home. Besides, she could not allow Josiah to witness such a scene. The child had already been through a nightmare without entering this place of death.

Betsy scanned her home—her refuge and comfort. No longer. This haven now held a terror that twisted her heart with unspeakable dread.

Windows everywhere were broken, the glass scattered about. She stopped to pick up a shard laying near her feet, held it up, and dropped it.

Blood!

She backed up several inches, pulling Josiah with her. "Do not touch anything on the ground, Josiah."

He remained silent as he nodded his head.

Glancing back toward the front door, she anxiously awaited her mother and Thomas' return.

That's when she saw it.

"Wait here, Josiah. I'll be back forthwith. I promise." She squeezed his hand to reassure him before she walked toward the granite slab that stepped up to her front door.

Only this was not the same grey granite that she had walked on at noon—was it just today? This granite was now dark red. Blood red.

She put her hand over her mouth, turned, and ran back toward Josiah. Clutching the boy, she waited for her mother to return and vowed never to walk on that step again.

It seemed they waited forever. In truth, Betsy knew it was but a few moments before her mother emerged from the house. She looked as if she had aged ten years in ten minutes. Shaking as if with the palsy, her mother's face had blanched so white it appeared she had been covered with wheat flour. Thomas helped her down the steps while Betsy watched.

Pity for her dear mother overwhelmed her.

Has she not been through enough loss?

Betsy's outrage at the British festered like a corrupt infection intent upon killing off any remnant of goodness in her heart.

She watched her mother slip out of her shoes and then absentmindedly wipe first one foot, then the other, on the blades of spring grass sprouting in the yard. She repeated the routine several times. Walking toward her mother, Betsy inquired, "Pray, Mother, what are you doing?"

"The blood." She met Betsy's concerned gaze. "The blood ...'tis ankle deep."

The ashen countenance of her only remaining parent horrified Betsy. "We shall clean it soon enough, Mother. Let us go rest. We shall return to the Prentiss' and sleep there tonight."

Coaxing her stricken mother, she wrapped one arm around her and led Josiah with the other hand, leading them both back to their haven—their refuge from this den of death.

"I count on you the most, Betsy. You may someday find yerself tremblin' with fear, lass, but trust in the Lord."

Her father's instructions echoed in her thoughts. She knew what she needed to do.

Lord, give me the strength to do it.

13

The troubles of my heart are enlarged:
O bring thou me out of my distresses.

Psalm 25:17

APRIL 19, 1775
10:00 PM

Betsy stared into the flickering hearth at the Prentiss house. Most of the women and children had returned to their homes.

Betsy was not sure what they would discover at their homecoming. She knew only that, in the wake of war, her house was uninhabitable for the living.

As dead as she felt in her spirit, perhaps her own home was a suitable abode for her, after all.

Her appetite escaped her. The only reason she drank the cider in Mrs. Prentiss' tankard was to squelch the raw, dry irritation in her throat. That sensation only kept her senses on edge. She preferred no reminders that she lived while so many others had died.

She lived, but her father was gone.

The tears she kept prisoner in her heart threatened to escape her jail of restraint. Once one prisoner broke out, a flood of mourning would surely follow.

She tightened her jaw and sniffed. No tears would bypass the barred doors of her tenacity.

The front door opened, and Betsy grabbed her pocket where she hid her knife. She tensed her arms, prepared to lunge out of the seat to protect her family. As she saw her brother Thomas, she exhaled in relief.

Hand on her chest, she breathed in deeply. "I vow, Thomas, you gave me a fright."

"Sorry, Betsy. I thought perhaps you were sleepin'. Didn't want to awaken anyone." He bent down and tenderly patted her cap. "How do you fare?"

He looked so exhausted. She could not fathom his concern for her well-being.

"Well enough. Sit down, Thomas. Let me fill a tankard with cider."

She struggled to her feet and went to the kettle on the hearth to pour some warm cider while her brother collapsed into the empty chair by the fire. He arched his shoulders and winced, rubbing his upper arms.

Betsy handed him the drink, staring with concern. "Are you injured, Thomas? Wounded?"

"Nay, Betsy. My body pains me from the day. Never did shoot a musket so many times before." He sipped the cider and closed his eyes in satisfaction. "The perfect drink. Thank you, Betsy." Leaning back in the chair, he extended his legs and stretched his lower limbs, continuing to wince. Finally settled back against the wooden slats, he sighed and stared at the fire.

Moments later, Thomas looked up abruptly. "Where is everyone?"

"Anna and the baby lie in the birthing room while Mrs. Hanscomb lies on the floor beside her. Mother shares Mrs. Prentiss' bed with her. Mr. Prentiss, Noah, and Josiah sleep in the barn."

Thomas relaxed into the chair again. "I fed the stock. 'Tis a surprise those lobsters did not steal them. Or kill them just for spite."

Betsy sat down again and shivered. "Just for spite?"

The regulars are animals!

"Aye." Thomas stared at the fire. "They were in too much of a hurry to get back to Boston, more'n likely."

They were both silent for several moments. Betsy sat forward, and the chair creaked on the wooden floor. "Thomas, tell me what happened." She could barely get the words out, but she wanted to know. She *had* to know.

It seemed an eternity as Thomas stared silently into the fire. The reflection of the flames flickered in his wide pupils, giving the appearance that his eyes were afire.

Finally, he blinked and spoke.

"It was just after dawn when we marched west toward Lexington. But we were too late to help them there." He swallowed. "Several of the butchers fired upon the militia standing on the green. Many never stood again." He took a quick gulp of cider and wiped his mouth on his sleeve.

"So our unit headed west again to Concord. This time, hundreds of Minutemen from all around had come together to fight Gage's brutes. And this time, we had the upper hand." He gave a slight smile as he focused on the flames in the hearth.

"We shot two of them and chased the rest across the bridge. It was a sight to see them running away from a bunch of colonial farmers.

"The regulars saw our numbers growin' by the minute. By noon, they started to retreat to Boston. Captain Locke told us to spread out and fight like Indians from behind stonewalls along the road. We kept strikin' at 'em from the sidelines before they knew what was about. Had 'em sweating rivers, I tell you. Kept followin' … firin'. Then, near Lexington, more bloody-backs showed up from Boston. Gage's reinforcements. Devils." He spat the words in disgust and shook his head. "These butchers were not so tired as our lobster 'friends' from Concord. And they were angry. You could see it in their faces."

Thomas paused for several moments and stared, his gaze fixed and somber.

Betsy waited in anticipation, but Thomas seemed reluctant to go on. Finally, she could stand to wait no more.

"And then? What happened, Thomas?"

"Then, the demons of hell appeared in the guise of the king's army." His hand rubbed across his eyes as if to erase the memory. "Once they got past the Foot of the Rocks, they began entering the houses all along the road."

Betsy set her tankard of cider on a small table and gripped the arms of her chair. Blood rushed through her ears as Thomas continued.

"Robbins' house on Pierce's Hill was ransacked and set afire. There was so much wet clothing hanging to dry it helped save the house from complete demise. The family had fled, praise be to a merciful God.

"Tuft's Tavern was pillaged and nearly destroyed by fire. Bloody-backs took what they could carry, then opened up all the casks of molasses and spirits. If Cutler's slave had not seen the destruction from a safe distance, the place would have been completely lost."

Thomas continued. "Then Deacon Adams' place ..."

Betsy shivered and hugged herself. "Mrs. Adams ... and the baby?" Her stomach roiled with nausea.

"They are safe but were nearly killed. I guess one bloody-back had a conscience and spared the woman and child, though she had to wrap herself in a blanket and crawl to the corn crib. They set the house afire, but her other children hid under the bed. They came out and doused the flames with ale." Thomas looked up at his sister. "They stole the communion service—even the silver tankard."

Betsy's heart pounded. "The sacred utensils?"

"Aye."

They were silent for a moment.

"Cooper's Tavern was an unconscionable massacre."

"Pray, what do you mean?" Betsy held her hand to her forehead, which throbbed.

Thomas paused a moment. "Benjamin and Rachel Cooper escaped to the cellar. But Cousin Jason and his brother-in-law Jabez were killed most mercilessly."

Betsy stuttered and blinked. "They ... they were armed?"

"Nay."

Betsy's head spun, but she resolved to know what had happened at their home. She inhaled a shuddering breath. "Pray, tell me. What terrible thing happened at our home?"

Thomas paused for so long Betsy feared she would never know. "Tell me!"

He startled at her vehement tone. "I shall tell you, so long as you do not share this with Mother."

"I promise." She leaned forward and locked her eyes with his.

"Father … Father had set up a breastwork of sorts at the gate. Wooden shingles that he thought could be a defense. He did not realize there is no defense against tyranny and rage.

"Before our unit got to Menotomy, I could see the troops were out of control. Some of the officers tried to retreat in formation, but it was useless—there was no controlling the armed mob. Other officers urged on their brutal behavior."

Even in the firelight, Betsy could see Thomas pale.

"By now, units from all over—Beverly, Danvers, Watertown—were swarming throughout Menotomy, trying to maintain their advantage. But some of our Minutemen were not familiar with flank-guards patrolling off to the side, often out of sight until 'twas too late."

Thomas rubbed his face with an open palm from forehead to chin.

"When the lads from Beverly and Danvers saw they were trapped, they ran toward our house trying to make a stand. That's when Father ran toward the front door…" He took in a quivering breath and his voice broke. "They slaughtered an old, lame man on his doorstep." Thomas covered his face and wept.

Betsy's eyes widened and brimmed with moisture. She covered her mouth with her hand.

I will not cry. If I start, I shall surely never cease.

Thomas wiped the moisture from his face.

"The bloody-backs were not content just to kill an old man. They were savages, bursting through the front door and running after the men from Beverly who ducked down in the cellar. These lads had their muskets pointing at the top of the stairs, and the first lobster that tried to descend got his just reward. Those men survived." He paused a moment.

"The Danvers men were not so fortunate. Let's just say it was a massacre of the worst kind. Muskets, bayonets, pistols, knives, hatchets—everything was used until not one of those men survived. One lobster fell as well."

Thomas' eyes looked vacant, dark, as if all life were released from them through the telling of such horror.

"The fighting continued out to the orchard. More dead militia. More dead soldiers wearing red. This time their red coats were mixed with their red blood." Thomas exhaled slowly. "I can speak of this no more."

Betsy sat in stunned silence. Thomas stared at the flames.

"I never wish to speak of this again." With that, Thomas drank the last gulp of cider, stood up, and walked out the door, closing it carefully. Betsy followed him and started to open the latch. She stopped when she heard an unfamiliar sound.

Thomas wept outside. But this was no ordinary cry of mourning. This was the heart-stopping wail of someone who had seen such horror that his entire body retched with sobs—sobs that choked him with every breath and tore apart his soul.

In all her life, she had never heard him cry. In truth, she had never heard anyone cry as Thomas did. But then, this was no ordinary day. And Betsy knew that more tears would be shed by men who had perhaps not wept since they were children, men who would never look at their world the same again.

Betsy bowed her head as she released the prisoner of grief locked up in her heart. She freed her own tears of sorrow for the innocence of everyone now lost forever.

14

Betsy stirred the corn gruel in the Prentiss' kettle. Although the coals in the hearth glowed steadily, the heat from the embers did little to warm her. She had barely gotten any sleep in the chair.

Mrs. Prentiss came out of her bedchamber and carefully shut the door. Tiptoeing toward the main room where Betsy worked, she whispered, "Yer mother finally fell asleep, poor one." Glancing at the kettle, she smiled slightly. "Ye didna' have to start the meal, dear Betsy."

"I needed to take a turn for you, to redeem the debt for all you've done for us, Mrs. Prentiss."

The woman placed a gentle hand on her shoulder.

"Betsy, ye know there is no 'takin' a turn' in repayment during such a time as this. We're all leanin' on each other to survive."

Betsy attempted to smile in gratitude, but her mouth trembled instead. "'Tis most kind, Mrs. Prentiss."

The older woman pulled Betsy's chin upward toward her wrinkled face. "'Tis the way of it during war, Betsy." The pale eyes of the woman glistened, and she turned her head aside. "Well then, let me take some of these victuals to our new mother in the birthin' room."

Once again, Betsy had forgotten about the new life that had emerged. "I'll take some to Anna, Mrs. Prentiss." She ladled a heaping mound of gruel into a trencher and carried the warm bowl toward the birthing room. She gently knocked on the door and awaited Anna's voice before she leaned against it and entered.

"Ah, some food. I am quite famished." Anna licked her lips and put her arms up to take the wooden bowl. Betsy looked over at her new niece, whom Mrs. Hanscomb now cleaned. Leaning closely to look at the baby's face, Betsy noticed a fluff of thick brown hair on her head.

"I vow, her hair looks like Thomas'!" Betsy almost cracked a smile.

"Aye, true enough." Anna grinned. "She looks much like her father."

Anna devoured the corn gruel while Betsy watched in surprise. As she took the empty bowl from Anna so that Mrs. Hanscomb could place the infant back in her arms, Betsy looked up to see her brother enter. "Thomas. Did you sleep in the barn?"

"Aye." Thomas' voice was thick and sleepy. He leaned down and kissed Anna and the baby.

"Thomas, what shall we name her?" Anna stroked the soft cheek of the infant, who moved her head back and forth in search of her own breakfast.

"I think she should be called 'Anna.' If she is even half as lovely as her mother, she will bear the name well."

Anna blushed. "Thank you, Thomas." The baby began to cry and Anna grinned. "'Tis time for her to eat."

"Then I shall let you feed her whilst I get my gruel. I'll return forthwith, Anna. There is much to be done in ..." He lowered his eyes to the hat that he gripped with white knuckles. "There is much to be done."

He exited the room and Betsy followed.

"Thomas, pray, will you not sit and stay a bit?"

Thomas looked up with bleary, swollen eyes. "As soon as I've eaten, I must go help in the town."

"Then I shall go with you."

He sighed, then rubbed his fatigued face. "I could use your help. Mother should stay here."

Betsy nodded with a determined resignation that she did not feel. She never wanted to face the horror that hovered over every home in her town. What she really wished she could do was run away into the woods. But that was a dream. Instead, she would have to face the nightmare.

After serving up breakfast for Thomas, she poured him some coffee. Betsy sampled a taste of the dark liquid. It was a bitter brew, perfect for a day filled with the harshness of facing the aftermath of war.

A bitter day indeed.

Mrs. Prentiss came in from outdoors, carrying a bucket of milk. "There now, that's done."

Betsy spoke up. "Mrs. Prentiss, Thomas and I are going down the hill to help ... clean up. Can Josiah stay with you? He may be frightened upon awakening."

Mrs. Prentiss smiled and stroked some hair that had fallen out of Betsy's cap. "Of course, child. Think no more of the lad. He'll be safe here with me. And I'll let yer sweet mother lie abed as long as she will." The woman pulled Betsy into her arms and hugged her. "Ye be brave now, lass."

Betsy wanted to collapse in the comfort of the woman's consoling arms. Instead, she stiffened and forced a strained smile. "Aye, Mrs. Prentiss. Thank you."

Thomas stood from the table, leaving a half-empty bowl, and tipped his hat at Mrs. Prentiss. "Thank you, madam."

She nodded and Betsy thought she saw a damp trail trickle down the woman's cheek. Turning away lest her own tears emerge, Betsy grabbed her shawl and followed Thomas.

The coolness of the morning air prompted Betsy to inhale deeply. The bolstering breath filled her lungs with unexpected energy. She needed every bit of strength she could muster. Walking with boldness down the steep incline, she hastened her steps to catch up with her brother.

"Thomas?"

He stopped and looked back at her. "Aye?"

"Have they ... have they removed all the bodies?"

He sighed. "I know not." He met her eyes intently. "Are you able to do this, Betsy?"

She forced herself to stand tall, despite her unsteady legs. "Aye, Thomas. I shall do my part."

His eyes admired her. "You are your father's daughter." He squeezed her arm. "Let us be off then."

No one had ever said that to her before: *Your father's daughter.*

It filled her with hope—hope that she could do the right thing. The necessary thing. The brave thing. Even if it meant looking into the face of death.

The closer that Betsy and Thomas got to Concord Road, the faster her heart beat. Activity bustled everywhere, yet few voices suffused the air. The stench of old rags set to wash after soaking up blood assaulted Betsy's nostrils and she covered her nose.

Yet there was another, more horrible smell. It brought to mind the wretched odor of a dead animal that she and Noah had once found in the woods. The overwhelming attack on her senses halted her steps a moment as she attempted to control the dizziness in her head.

Thomas had noticed the stench as well and stopped to pull a kerchief from his pocket, which he tied around his nose. With shaking hands, Betsy pulled the linen kerchief from around her neck and did the same.

They paused a moment and looked at each other before trudging once again toward the Russell house. Neither attempted to speak through the woven cloth.

Nearing her home, Betsy slowed her pace when she saw two men carrying a body down the front steps and across the grass to a cart. At least she assumed they carried a man. The stiffened form was unrecognizable, completely painted with a dark red coating that obscured any features or folds of clothing. Betsy turned away when the man's queue fell away from the body, the motion of the transport shaking it loose from its plaster of blood. Betsy's breakfast churned in her stomach.

The two oxen yoked to the wagon chewed on the tall foliage, oblivious to the somber task they were drafted to perform. The weary workers, covered with splotches of rusty red, laid the dead Minuteman across several bodies already in the cart.

Ammi Cutter came running across the road carrying a sheet. "Where be your honorable father, lad?" He gripped Thomas' arm. The young man patted the elder's arm.

"I know not." His kerchief sucked in toward his mouth as he spoke. "I shall find him." Looking at Betsy, he motioned for her to remain where she stood.

Thomas trudged like an old man toward the door. He met the workers—fellow militia—and asked them a question Betsy could not hear. The men pointed inside. Thomas turned toward Mr. Cutter and motioned him to come with him.

Betsy hugged her shawl tightly around her shoulders. Once again she waited in her yard, afraid to enter her home.

In a few moments, the four men carried out a body wrapped in the sheet Mr. Cutter had brought. Unspeakable sorrow gripped Betsy's chest. She pulled the kerchief from her face and let the tears roll unhindered. Walking toward the body, she followed the men to the wagon.

Thomas noticed her as the men lifted it into the cart. "Betsy, stand back."

She ignored her brother's command and approached the stack of bodies. Reaching toward the shrouded form, she touched her father and sobbed at his stiffness.

"Betsy, no!" Her brother grabbed her arm.

"Father ..." She shook off Thomas' grip and touched the long, gray hair that had slipped from under the sheet. She gingerly combed her fingers through the blood-splattered strands while her tears showered the locks with her grief.

One of the Minutemen cried unashamedly. He gently removed Betsy's grip from her dead father's hair. After removing a hunting knife from his sheath, he took a small bundle of Jason Russell's hair, cut off several inches of the silver queue, and handed it to her.

She stared silently at the locks in her hand and closed her grip around them.

Oh, that this hair were still a part of my living, breathing father! How can I bear to part with his life? His love? His protection? Dear Father in heaven this is too difficult—my heart is breaking!

A gentle breeze stirred the gray strands in her fingers as an unexpected and strange calm flooded her being.

The sharp sniffing of the crying soldier drew her attention.

Lifting her gaze, she struggled to compose herself. With great effort, she blurted out, "Thank you."

The man's lips trembled. He tried to answer. Unable, he looked down, put his knife away, and returned to Betsy's house for the next body.

Mr. Cutter's grief-stricken face twisted in torment. "They tried to kill us both. I tripped and fell, and the bloody-backs thought I was dead." He shook his head slowly, then covered his face with trembling fingers. "They never gave yer father a chance. Why was I the one spared? They should 'a killed me, too!"

Thomas put his hand on the old man's shoulder, his voice barely above a whisper. "Thank you for the shroud, Mr. Cutter."

His deep-set eyes glistened with tears as he stared at Thomas. "I could not stand for my good friend to be laid in his grave without so much as a sheet to cover him."

Thomas stared at the ground. "I am most grateful."

*   *   *

Workers at the burying ground dug one huge grave for all twelve men. There was little time to prepare hand-sewn shrouds or wooden boxes in which to lay the bodies. There was a war to prepare for.

Betsy stood still, like a statue she had once seen in Boston, her limbs as lifeless as chiseled stone. She wished she were without life and that she could not feel the pain of such loss. So inanimate was she, Betsy wondered if the mourners nearby might assume she belonged in the grave next to the patriotic martyrs. Would she care if they threw her in amongst them? Would they see on the outside what she felt inside—that a part of her had died forever?

She stood by the huge, open grave next to her mother, her brothers Thomas and Noah, and her nephew, Josiah. The townsmen took their turn pouring in shovelfuls of dark earth over the bodies. Betsy covered her nose with a kerchief that she had soaked in lavender water. The floral scent did little to soothe her heart.

An entire field of sweet lavender could not hide the scent of death. Nor the pain of it.

Josiah's fingers trembled as he reached up to hold her hand.

Although his grip comforted her and stoked warmth into her soul, she mourned for the happier Josiah of days gone by—the Josiah who thought he was too grown up to hold anyone's hand.

Will he ever know comfort again? Shall I?

Staring blankly at the burial scene, she was surprised by a familiar voice from behind calling, "Josiah!"

Betsy turned on her heels, as did the seven-year-old.

"Father!" Josiah released his aunt's hand and raced into Jason's arms. Betsy's brother swept his son into his arms and hugged him as if he would never let go. When he let Josiah down to the ground, Jason turned toward Betsy and the others.

Their mother stumbled into the arms of her oldest son. Jason held his grieving mother and, through his own tears, explained his presence. "We heard about what happened here—the battle. About Father. I came forthwith from Mason—rode out at dawn this morning."

Betsy approached her brother with stiffened steps. "We're so glad to see you, Jason. Josiah missed you terribly." She squeezed his arm.

Josiah tugged on his father's sleeve. "Father, Aunt Betsy watched out for me when the bloody-backs came through Menotomy."

Jason grinned. "I'm certain she did." He looked at his sister. "Thank you. With all my heart, I'm grateful you took care of my son."

"I would ne'er let any harm befall this precious one." She stroked Josiah's head.

"My own Elizabeth was beside herself when we heard the news. I must hasten home with Josiah so she knows he's safe."

Betsy hugged herself with clenched fingers. The ache of yet another loss replaced the brief joy of seeing her brother. Josiah was leaving her.

"Of course." She cleared her throat. "His mother must be desperate to see him."

"Do stay for supper, Jason." Their mother begged him to consider the offer as she gently touched her son's arm.

Jason reached out to her. "Nay, Mother. There's talk of more war here in Massachusetts. I must return as soon as possible to New Hampshire. I am under pressure to join up with the militia."

"The militia? Pray, why?" Betsy could not understand why he would feel so compelled to join—a man in his thirties with numerous children.

Her brother cleared his throat. "Well, it has to do with a certain cow belonging to our Tory reverend. The cow met an early demise and for some reason, some believe that *I* had something to do with it."

Betsy squinted with a doubtful look. "Pray, for what reason, dear brother, would they suspect you?" She knew Jason all too well.

He looked at her and winked. "I shall be joining up with Captain Mann forthwith."

"Well then, you shall be the finest-dressed militiaman with your wife's weaving." Betsy's teasing banter quickly faded as she saw Jason staring at the newly-turned grave where their father lay.

Her brother's expression fell, the joy of the reunion now overshadowed by the reality of yesterday's events.

"I must …" He swallowed visibly. "I would like a moment alone."

"Of course." Thomas led the group away. The oldest brother walked closer to the grave and lingered for several moments.

Betsy took in a deep breath and drew Josiah aside.

Squatting down, she looked him in the eye. "Josiah, you must always remember to be strong. To help your mother at home. To say your prayers."

"Yes, Aunt Betsy." His lip quivered.

Her voice nearly caught in her throat. "You and I, we have shared a moment in time unlike any other." She could barely swallow, there were so many tears in her throat. "I shall always remember how brave you were. How you helped me to be brave."

He rubbed his damp eyes. "I helped *you*?"

"Aye. You're my brave hero, young man."

He cried openly now.

"Aunt Betsy, I'll miss you."

She grabbed him and held him close.

"And I'll miss you more than you can imagine."

Footsteps approached from behind as Jason returned from the graveside.

"Betsy, Josiah and I must hasten. His mother awaits."

Betsy stood and let go of the boy. Wiping tears away with impatient fingers, she sniffed. "Aye, Jason. 'Tis so." She squeezed Josiah's shoulder one last time and inhaled deeply. "Godspeed, Josiah." Her moist eyes threatened to burst like a dam after a rain. "Remember what I said."

"I shall, Aunt Betsy." He took a few steps away, then whipped around and ran into her arms. They held each other tightly for a moment before she released him with reluctance.

"Go with your father, Josiah."

He pulled away, reached up and kissed her cheek, and ran after Jason.

Betsy turned and ran into the woods, covering her mouth to quell the sobs. She had survived the battle and helped keep Josiah safe, only to have to let him go.

Dear God, my heart cannot bear this pain—it will surely break. This burden is too great.

Pouring her heart out before God, she recalled what Reverend Cooke once said. They were words spoken by God to the Apostle Paul when his burden was too great: *"My grace is sufficient for thee: for my strength is made perfect in weakness."*

15

O, to awaken on a Sabbath morn and be renewed with joy. Verily, joy mocks at my heart this day as it waves farewell forever.

~ Diary of Betsy Russell, 23 April 1775

APRIL 23, 1775
SABBATH MORNING

Menotomy's roadway bore as many scars as its inhabitants. The surface of Concord Road had been marred by thousands of marching British soldiers and pitted from the explosive blasts of their cannons.

Those who remained of the Russell household—Betsy, her brother Noah, and their mother—picked their way to the meetinghouse, treading carefully on the pock-marked dirt pathway.

Drawing closer to their destination, Betsy saw Thomas step out of his storefront. He held baby Anna, who would be baptized today, the sole shining moment for the family on this day of mourning.

Silence hung over the residents approaching the meetinghouse. Usually early spring weather elicited an abundance of chatter among the neighbors. But today, with so many missing, heartache lingered within the congregation, quenching the usual day-to-day conversation. Grim faces met Betsy's eyes as she watched one family after another trudging toward the building. Every household missed at least one member. Some were missing more. Staring at the vacant places in her family pew, Betsy's heart ached.

Thomas held the wooden pew door open so they could easily slide onto the long seat. The latch closed with a sharp click. It echoed the emptiness. There was too much room on the cold bench, and Betsy shivered. She longed to sense her father's warm presence beside her, providing a comfort that, up until now, she had taken for granted. She stared straight ahead, hoping to focus on anything except her losses.

After the congregation took their seats, silence filled the room. A pew squeaked as someone adjusted his or her position. Otherwise, few signs of life occurred in the usually animated meetinghouse.

Betsy stared at her hands, smoothing a finger across the red and rough skin that bled from cracks. Harsh vinegar and days spent cleaning the floors in the Russell home had done their damage. But, even after repeated scrubbing with the acidic liquid, the wooden slats that had cradled the bodies of twelve dead men never seemed clean. While Noah said he only smelled vinegar, Betsy could only smell blood.

The sound of plodding footsteps drew Betsy's attention. A solemn-faced Reverend Cooke climbed into the pulpit. Resting a hand on each edge of the podium, he stared at his open Bible without speaking. When he began to preach, his voice captured the attention of the congregation with its strength and boldness.

"We who are left in Menotomy must carry the torch so boldly borne by our fallen comrades. Their sacred blood dost water the earth with cries that shout to the living, 'Stand firm in thy resolve. Let not thine enemy darken the light of our hope.' Thus, let that hope be our shield to carry against those that delight in our blood.

"Scatter them, O Lord! For the sighing of the oppressed and needy, make bare Thine almighty arm for their help. Teach our hands to war. Ah, and our fingers to fight, since in Thy providence we are called to this!"

As a small, wrinkled woman stood up, all eyes in the meetinghouse drew to her.

"Mother Batherick!" Reverend Cooke outstretched his arm to the woman who stood straight and tall. "Our most venerable warrior, who, though aged and frail, single-handedly took prisoner six of the crown's highly-trained soldiers. An anthem of tribute should proclaim your bravery to the world, madam."

The woman looked around the congregation with fire in her eyes. "There I was, digging up the dandelions growing in my garden, when six cowards of the king approached me." Her finger pointed to emphasize her words. "Gage's troops surrendering to an old woman, begging for my protection."

She shook her head in disgust. "When I delivered my prisoners to Captain Frost, I looked at the pathetic lot and said, 'If you ever live to get back, you tell King George that an old woman took six of his grenadiers prisoner.'" She nodded sharply and sat back down.

"Hear, hear!" Several of the men in the congregation shouted their approval.

Betsy stared in awe at the woman who had a composed expression, as though this was a normal church announcement. Betsy recalled the story of the regulars escaping from David Lamson and his men firing upon them at the bridge. She had heard of the frightened survivors surrendering to Mother Batherick while she gardened. The story was, even now, astonishing.

Such bravery!

Others stood up, one by one, sharing their own tales of the previous Wednesday. Though not a typical Sabbath service, Betsy realized it was the congregation's way of supporting each other in their losses and celebrating in the few victories they had.

The townspeople inhaled sharply at the story of Samuel Whittemore. Though eighty years old, he had refused to hide with the women and children. He had taken cover behind a stone wall and, after killing or wounding three enemy soldiers, he was shot in the head, stabbed with bayonets thirteen times, and left for dead.

Rage thickened Betsy's blood.

The sheer wickedness of attacking such an old man!

Although surgeons thought it pointless to dress Mr. Whittemore's wounds, they decided to cover them anyway. On this Sabbath Day, everyone rejoiced that he yet lived to see another sunrise.

Betsy's mouth tightened, and her exhausted body felt energized by the bitter thoughts.

I shall never forgive these butchers for their savagery.

Even as decisive anger coursed through her veins, the uncomfortable edge of conscience pricked at her spirit. She pushed it away as she would a threatening dagger. She wanted to wallow in her bitterness. She would never forgive what they had done to her father.

Her anger was interrupted by her brother, Thomas, who stood with his daughter in his arms. He opened the small portal to the pew and brought little Anna toward the front of the meetinghouse.

The widow of Jason Winship brought her young son forward, as well. The sight of both babies—one without her grandfather, one without his father—brought communal tears to the congregation.

Betsy could barely focus on Reverend Cooke's words as he sprinkled water over the tops of the children's heads. Both infants screamed at the application of the water that the minister declared was the "sacred covenant of baptism." Betsy cried along with the little ones in their parents' arms.

Little Anna was now wailing loudly, so Thomas exited the building to take the child home to her mother. Mrs. Winship took her little one outside.

The closing prayer must have already been spoken, because the congregation was now standing for the final hymn. Betsy stood with unsteady legs and leaned against the pew in front of her. Rather than sing, she closed her eyes.

I shall never forget.

Mercifully, the music stopped quickly. Most of the congregants appeared too grief-stricken to sing, so after only two choruses of "A Mighty Fortress is Our God," everyone shuffled toward the exit. Betsy made every effort to forget that it was always her father who held the pew door open for the whole family. She hurried past the open door that swung on its hinge, as if awaiting her father's firm grasp.

She tightened the grip on her shawl and hurried to her mother's side to help support her arm. Her mother had spoken little since Wednesday. Betsy feared for the grief-stricken widow.

Will she ever be the same? Will I?

A dark cloud of gloom—like a physical manifestation—swarmed Betsy's mind and soul. Its shadow hovered over her every thought, her every movement. Even her gait seemed stiff and inflexible.

She was shaken out of her deep despair by the sight of a woman hurrying toward the townspeople leaving the meetinghouse.

"Can you help me, please? I cannot take care of the man all day and night. I need some help!"

She begged for assistance. One by one, she approached each family with waving arms and earnest pleas. Each family shook their head "no" and walked away.

Betsy's eyes narrowed.

Of whom does Mrs. Butterfield speak?

Thomas had arrived back at the church to assist his mother on the half-mile walk home. As Betsy released her mother's arm to the care of her brother, Mrs. Butterfield approached her, nearly in tears. The middle-aged woman looked as if she had not slept in days. Her slightly graying hair came undone beneath the lower edges of her lace mobcap, and her apron was filthy with blood.

Betsy was shocked at the appearance of the normally refined woman.

"Mrs. Butterfield."

The woman grabbed Betsy's arm in desperation. "Please … Miss Russell, I need someone's help." Glancing toward the now-widowed Elizabeth Russell, who walked with difficulty toward home, Mrs. Butterfield gripped Betsy even tighter. "I am so aggrieved about your dear father." Tears welled in Mrs. Butterfield's eyes. "Is your mother recovering?"

Betsy glanced downward. "I am certain she will recover." It seemed the right thing to say, but Betsy was not certain of the truth of it.

The woman's eyes were pleading and her voice trembled. "Forgive my desperation, Miss Russell. I vow I have not slept in days."

Searching the woman's eyes, Betsy clearly saw Mrs. Butterfield's exhaustion. "Pray, how can I help?"

"There are two wounded soldiers in my home. I found them there upon my return from hiding during the battle." She swallowed, then inhaled unevenly. "One of them recovers, but the second one … the doctor feels his wounds are mortal."

Betsy felt a small stirring of compassion. "How can I help you? Do you need linens, food? Pray, tell me."

"All of these, lass. But mostly, I need a nurse to help tend to the dying man."

Betsy recoiled at the thought. But looking at the strain on poor Mrs. Butterfield, she knew she needed to help the woman.

"I shall make certain that Mother is well-looked after. Then I shall bring you some victuals and linens. I'll not leave you to carry this burden alone, Mrs. Butterfield." An unsettling thought crossed her mind. "Pray, why do the others all deny you assistance? I don't understand."

Mrs. Butterfield released Betsy's arm and folded both her arms across her breasts. Looking away into the distance, she was silent for a moment. Sighing with resignation, she looked back at Betsy. "They already know who the dying man is."

Betsy tilted her head in confusion. "I know not what you mean."

Appearing to gather her courage, Mrs. Butterfield took a deep breath. "The dying man is a king's soldier."

Betsy gasped and grabbed her shawl. Whipping around, she clenched her fists on the wool and breathed in deeply. It was only her mother's words of admonition to be God-fearing and polite that kept her from screaming at the woman.

All the other congregants had left for their homes. A spring breeze whipped the ribbons on Betsy's bonnet. They tickled her face, and she used one finger to pull them angrily away.

If she thinks I will help her!

Turning on her heels, she prepared to decline as politely as she could, but she saw Mrs. Butterfield's face in her hands. The woman was weeping inconsolably.

Betsy's anger melted at the sight. She walked over to her and lightly touched her arm. "Mrs. Butterfield. Please forgive me. I was so shocked."

The woman shook her head. "Nay, forgive me for askin'. You, of all the lasses to ask. What was I thinkin'? Everyone is callin' me a Tory. I'm certain you think that of me, as well."

Betsy wrapped her arm around the weeping woman. "Nay, Mrs. Butterfield. I've known you all my life. Never would I believe that of you."

The older woman looked up through her tears. "I came home from hiding out Wednesday last. There were two men in my bedchamber, one in each bed. Both wounded, both bleedin' all through the bed covers. One was our own militia. One wore a coat of red." She sobbed erratically. "How could I care for one and not the other? I did not pay mind to what army they served. I just saw they both shed the same blood. I knew that God would not wish me to shed my compassion, despite the causes of men."

Despite the causes of men.

Betsy could not shake away the words.

Dear Lord, how can I do this? You ask too much of me!

The trickle of rage in her heart threatened to become a flood of retaliation.

But the words she had learned from her parents through the years held back the flood like a dam of conviction: *Love thine enemies.*

Try as she might, she could not ignore the precepts so deeply imbedded in her soul. Taking in a breath of pure resolve, despite her deepest desires to resist, Betsy said, "I shall help you, Mrs. Butterfield."

The woman's mouth gaped in astonishment and then her eyes lit up with joy. "Thank you, dear Miss Russell." She grabbed Betsy and hugged her briefly. "My dear, God will bless you for your kindness in ways you could never imagine."

Betsy barely smiled at Mrs. Butterfield. "I know 'tis what God would want me to do." She paused. "Let me attend to my mother to make sure she's well. Then I shall gather a few things to bring over."

Betsy realized that, even if she could not feel compassion for this enemy soldier, her heart could easily reach out to help this exhausted neighbor.

She also knew that it would take a miracle of the greatest proportions to help her feel any sympathy for the enemy in Mrs. Butterfield's bedchamber.

That will never occur.

16

If thine enemy be hungry, give him bread to eat; and if he be thirsty, give him water to drink.

Proverbs 25:21

APRIL 23, 1775
SABBATH AFTERNOON

"Betsy, do not do this!" Thomas threw the bundle of wood in a heap near the hearth. "Mrs. Butterfield has taken on a task that everyone else deems dangerous and treasonous to our cause."

"Treasonous? Thomas, she is helping a dying man."

His response unnerved her. "He is a dying bloody-back!"

The rage in Thomas' eyes frightened her. Must she deal with her own anger as well as her brother's?

Betsy's heart raced so fast, she thought she might faint. A salty taste flooded her tongue as tears threatened to overtake her. "Thomas, I promised Mrs. Butterfield. Please…" Her words caught in her throat. This was difficult enough without such resistance from her own brother.

"Mrs. Butterfield is a Tory!" Thomas stood with his hands on his hips, glaring at her.

"Thomas, she is not. You know her as well as I do." Betsy's strained voice sounded small through the pounding pulse in her ears.

"Love thine enemies." Her mother spoke for the first time the entire day. Her voice, quieter than her usual tenor, infused words of clarity and calm into the room. She narrowed her eyes and captured Thomas with the look on her face.

Forced to back down in order to honor his remaining parent, Thomas gently pleaded his case. Elizabeth put her hand up—the signal to arrest any argument.

He threw his hands up toward the ceiling. "There is no reasoning with you!" Whipping around toward Betsy again, he looked at her accusingly. "And who will take care of Mother and Noah?"

Elizabeth slowly stood with a fortitude she had not shown in days. "I shall take care of us." She shuffled over to the fire, bent down for a piece of wood, and threw it into the fire.

Mother is back!

Betsy placed her hands together in front of her mouth and smiled. "Mother, are you certain you can manage?"

Mother looked up from stirring the kettle of soup that Betsy had prepared. "I'll manage well enough. Thank you, Betsy." Reaching over toward her daughter's arm, she touched it lightly. "You make me proud—helping Mrs. Butterfield."

Thomas huffed and prepared to leave. He turned at the open doorway and pointed to the two women. "Do not be shocked if someone paints your chimney white!"

A look of horror crossed Betsy's face at the implication.

Would someone truly believe we were Tories? Would we be at risk of losing our stock? Or even worse—perhaps our very lives?

Her mother chuckled.

Betsy opened her mouth in astonishment. "Mother! 'Tis not a trifling thing to have a white chimney, to be deemed a Tory!"

Life erupted in her mother's eyes—more than Betsy had seen in days. "Betsy, do you think the town will truly think we are the enemy? After seeing what the British did to your father?" Her countenance fell and tears welled. "'Tis one thing to follow what's right on this earth, to take a stand against an unjust cause. 'Tis another altogether to forget the precepts of God when there is a person in need. We must look past the horizon on earth at those times to view the horizon of heaven. God commands us to do so."

Betsy nearly forgot her resolve to remain bitter. Hugging her mother, she gathered the basket filled with linens, bread, and some hyssop that had been grown in the garden to make a healing tea.

"I shall be back soon, Mother. Pray, you *will* send Noah for me if you require my help, will you not?"

"I shall, lass. Go." Her mother shooed her out the door. Betsy nearly stepped on the front stoop, the last traces of blood now cleansed away. It was back to its former slate-gray color. Still, her foot stopped in mid-air.

"I think I shall go out the back door, Mother." She spun on her heels and hurried through the main room to the back of the house.

Plodding through the thick grass in the yard, she tried to avoid the areas where soldiers had died. It somehow seemed an abomination to step where their patriotic blood had flowed.

Making her way through the front gate, Betsy's thoughts grew troubled. She was not inclined to deal with illness well—certainly not mortal wounds. Her knowledge of nursing was confined to treating mild fevers that afflicted Noah or an occasional scrape or cut. But wounds from a musket? Betsy shivered. What would it even look like? She would rather not know.

Throwing her shoulders back stubbornly, she vowed that it did not truly matter. He was just the enemy, after all. Best he should be dying rather than live to kill her family and friends. Her soured countenance greeted Mrs. Butterfield when the woman answered the door.

Mrs. Butterfield narrowed her tired eyes. "Is all well, Miss Russell? Are you still able to help?"

"Oh, aye, Mrs. Butterfield. I … I was just in deep thought." Forcing a smile, Betsy shivered at what lay inside. "Shall I help you with the patients?"

The woman motioned Betsy in and offered to take her shawl. Reluctantly, Betsy gave the woolen wrap to Mrs. Butterfield but watched where it was hung.

I may wish to find it in a hurry. Perhaps I cannot tolerate the presence of this devil in the form of a man. I may need to escape.

Mrs. Butterfield sighed. "There is only one patient remaining, Miss Russell. Family came and brought Mr. Hemenway to his home to recover."

Betsy cleared her throat. "So, only the king's soldier remains?"

"Aye." The woman spoke with weariness. "Lieutenant Hall lies within. For now."

Moving toward the bedchamber, Betsy inhaled a breath for bravery, stood up tall, and followed the woman. She tripped once on an uneven floorboard and managed to catch herself.

Calm yourself, Betsy!

Entering the bedchamber, Betsy took wary steps toward the patient. The scent of lavender sprigs hanging around the room only partially disguised the smell of blood. Would she never cease to be assaulted with that scent? It permeated everywhere these days.

The soldier lying in the bed was covered with a linen sheet. His exposed shoulders and pale face were moist but appeared relatively clean.

No doubt thanks to Mrs. Butterfield's care.

A huge bandage encompassed one shoulder. Another dressing encircled the same arm.

Since the soldier appeared to be asleep, Mrs. Butterfield whispered. "He received the arm wound in the battle at Concord. It was not so serious. But as a wounded officer, he was transported in a cart during the retreat. The horse being not the fastest, he was an open target for yet another musket ball. That one imbedded in his shoulder. The army doctor that came from Boston was not able to remove it without killing him outright."

So now he gets to die slowly. Betsy shuddered.

Mrs. Butterfield swallowed. "The doctor said 'tis just a matter of time. A few days, a week perhaps." The woman bit her lip as it trembled.

Is she truly so moved by this man's plight?

Betsy grew impatient. "How can I help you, Mrs. Butterfield?"

She touched Betsy's arm. "If you could sit in the chair and give him some laudanum when he awakens. The doctor has left it for his pain. He may thirst. He can have sips of ale or cider."

A waste of good ale and cider. I refuse to look at the man's face—a visage from hell, no doubt.

Mrs. Butterfield showed Betsy how much medicine to pour for his pain. Betsy paid minimal attention to her instructions.

Does it really matter? If I give him too much, he'll get his just reward that much quicker. If I do not give enough, well, perhaps he can suffer more. Like Father did.

Her expression fixed in firm, unforgiving resolve.

"I must go and rest, Miss Russell." The poor woman looked as if she would collapse. A wave of compassion broke through Betsy's bitterness.

"Please, Mrs. Butterfield. Call me Betsy. And please, do rest. I'll do my best to carry on with your capable nursing care."

The woman smiled and walked with difficulty to another bedchamber. It was only a moment before Betsy heard gentle snores from the next room.

Betsy hugged herself and shifted her feet. Noticing a book on the small table, she wandered over to take a closer look.

Pilgrim's Progress. *One of Father's favorites! How many evenings did he spend reading to us in front of the hearth?*

She tenderly picked up the volume and sat in the chair a few feet away from the enemy soldier. She'd only read for a few minutes before her eyes grew heavy. At one point, the book jerked in her hands in unison with her head.

Perhaps if I close my eyes for just a moment.

* * *

Gut-wrenching moans startled Betsy from her slumber. As she sat up straight, *Pilgrim's Progress* slipped to the floor with a thud.

Lord, please don't let Mrs. Butterfield awaken! She will wonder what I am about!

Pushing herself from the chair, she looked at the face of the enemy for the first time. His eyes clenched tightly and his legs shifted restlessly under the sheet. Whenever he moved his neck, his discomfort worsened, and he flinched and moaned even louder.

Grabbing the small pewter vial on the bedside table, Betsy poured the amount she thought Mrs. Butterfield had directed. She stretched her arm out and held it in front of his face. "Here."

His eyes snapped open at the sound of her voice. Without speaking, he brought his uninjured hand up to grasp the cup that held small portions of the narcotic. He shook so much, the contents spilled as soon as he tried to bring it to his mouth.

"Blast!" The expletive came out weakly. In defeat, he dropped the vial to the floor and appeared to give up.

Annoyed, Betsy stooped down to look for it. There it was—under the bed.

Upon retrieving the cup, she popped up to find herself staring into the man's blue eyes glazed with pain.

"Who are you?" The man seemed short of breath.

"I am Miss Elizabeth Russell. My family and friends call me Betsy. I am here to help Mrs. Butterfield." She paused. "You may call me Miss Russell."

Silence.

"I see." He squinted his eyes. "Might I ask for more medicine, Miss Russell?"

She looked at the empty vial. "Yes, of course," she said, keeping her tone flat and dispassionate.

Pouring another dose, she started to hand it to him again but thought better of repeating the fiasco.

"How … how does Mrs. Butterfield give you the laudanum?"

He looked at her with wary eyes. "She usually lets me sip it slowly while she holds the vial—and my head."

Betsy balked at the thought but gathered her emotions.

"Very well, then."

Leaning toward the man, she reached behind his head and carefully pulled him upward. He grimaced in pain and cried out.

"I am sorry, sir. I did not realize how painful …" She licked her lips as her mouth dried. "Is there another way?" She cleared her throat, hoping it would moisten.

After recovering from the abrupt and painful motion, he moistened his own lips and met her eyes. "Please, miss, just move my head slightly—and slowly."

"Yes, sir." She followed his instructions, and his lips curved around the edge of the vial, hungrily seeking the drink that would alleviate some of his pain. He swallowed with difficulty and closed his eyes as she removed the small cup.

"Thank you, miss."

Her eyes narrowed slightly. "You are … welcome."

She stood and watched him breathe deeply. After a moment, his tension ebbed.

The laudanum must be taking effect.

She walked back toward the chair.

"You do not wish to be here, do you, miss?"

The soldier's words cut through her conscience, but she shielded herself from the assault.

Turning toward him, her eyes met his. "Nay. I do not wish to be helping a soldier of the king. I am here only to help Mrs. Butterfield."

She swirled around toward the chair and sat down with a thump. She tried to read the book again, but the words danced with her rapid heartbeat.

His whispered voice pierced the stillness. "Well then. I guess we understand each other. I do not wish to be here either." He smiled, but it quickly faded. "At least you will get to go home."

His words grabbed her soul, but she resisted their grip.

"Well then, perhaps you should not have left your home." She sniffed and pretended to be caught up in her reading.

Silence. After a moment she looked up at him and saw with consternation that his vivid blue eyes were moist as they stared at her. "You do not understand, do you?" His voice was far more vulnerable than she imagined it would be.

"Pray, understand what?" She closed the heavy volume with a thud.

He blinked. "The way of things in England, miss." He shifted in the bed and grimaced.

What if I did not pour enough laudanum? Perhaps I should have paid more heed to Mrs. Butterfield's instructions.

She immediately resisted the thought and the guilt it brought to her mind.

"And how could I, sir, since I am a colonist? The most pathetic of persons in the king's eyes, I suppose, not worthy of English rights nor regarded as anyone more than a slave. A wretch whose home can be attacked and her goods devoured by an army of savages." She could hear her blood pulsing.

His eyes blazed. "Savages? And you think the savagery we witnessed at Concord did not sicken us to the very core?" He winced in pain then went on. "I saw … one of your militia raise his hatchet … on the very scalp of one of our wounded, cutting off his ears. The weapon went so deep, the surgeon could do nothing to help him." Tears rolled from his eyes onto the pillow. "And you call *us* savages?"

Betsy's eyebrows furrowed. "I know naught of this."

He wiped his moist face with the hand on his uninjured arm. "Well, miss, I am certain there is much you do not know." His eyes grew heavy. "I must sle …" Before he finished the sentence, he drifted into slumber.

Betsy stared at the wounded man. The dying man.

Swallowing past the lump that formed in her throat, she reopened *Pilgrim's Progress*.

But it was not the words she saw on the page anymore. Instead, it was the vision of a soldier in a red coat with a hatchet stuck in his skull.

17

Have I ever been so fatigued in my eighteen years? How can I be so young yet feel so aged? I should be thinking about my future—yet I fear perhaps it is gone forever. I fear my future is now past.

~ Diary of Betsy Russell, 24 April 1775

April 25, 1775
Tuesday Morning

Betsy spent much of Monday helping Mrs. Butterfield wash linens. The endless piles of bloodstained bandages and sheets were nauseating.

So far, Mrs. Butterfield had not asked her to help change the dressings on the wounds. But Betsy knew that request would come soon enough. The British officer grew weaker daily.

Waking at dawn on Tuesday, Betsy lay in bed at home, trying to forget the events of the last week. Visions of dead and wounded militia, the incessant scrubbing of blood-drenched floors, and the hyper-vigilant eyes of the survivors all haunted her waking hours as well as her nightmares. But now a new image forced its way into her thoughts— an unsettling picture planted while speaking with Mrs. Butterfield's patient. Betsy nearly retched whenever she thought of the soldier with the hatchet in his head.

Turning over onto her side and glancing out the window, she observed robins singing on the tree branch outside. Their lively, upbeat trill seemed out of place with the gloom in her heart.

Fatigue overwhelmed her. Pushing herself up from the bed, she thought she'd be waking Josiah after she dressed. Then she remembered that he had gone home to New Hampshire. Blinking away tears, she poured chilly water into her washbowl and splashed the liquid onto her face. Drying with a towel, she glanced into the looking glass and gasped at her image. Deep circles darkened her eyes, and her mouth drew downward into a strained expression.

Have I changed so much? I look more my mother's age!

Sighing, she put a gown on over her night shift, pinned her hair up in a knot on top of her head, and placed a linen work cap over the mass of hair. She used to enjoy her long, brown tresses. Now her hair weighed on her head like one more burden.

She slowly descended the curved stairs and found her mother already up, stirring the morning gruel.

"How do you fare, Betsy?" Her mother looked at her with concern.

"I am well, Mother."

Lying again. But I cannot tell her my true state of mind. Desperate. Lonely. Bitter.

Betsy grinned slightly. "Perfectly well."

Elizabeth served her a trencher of gruel. Betsy stared at the unappetizing porridge and gulped. Forcing herself to eat a bite, she smiled again.

"What will you do today, Mother?"

She swallowed another bite, and her stomach rebelled against the sustenance.

"Thomas has arranged for a lawyer to see to the estate. He will bring him by today."

Betsy stiffened. "The estate?"

"Aye. It must be attended to soon." Her mother scooped up a bowl of breakfast for herself and sat down at the tableboard with Betsy.

"Where be Noah?" Betsy glanced around.

"He is tending the livestock. He was up before dawn."

"So, what happens to the estate?" She swallowed with difficulty.

Her mother sipped a teacup filled with coffee. "Thomas says that in these situations the court generally allows the house to remain occupied by the widow." As she said the word widow, Betsy's mother fought back tears. "The house itself will eventually go to Noah."

Betsy's appetite ceased altogether. "Pray, what about daughters?" She gripped the edges of the table.

Her mother reached over and squeezed Betsy's hand. "You will always be able to stay here. When you marry, you will go to your own husband's home, of course." Her mother smiled reassuringly.

Betsy's mouth trembled. "And what if I never marry?"

Her mother seemed astonished. "Of course you shall, Betsy. Why ever do you ask such a question?"

"Perhaps because I am not fair, like other maids. Nor ... nor ... desirable." Betsy pushed her chair away from the table and stood. "I must go help Mrs. Butterfield." Grabbing her shawl, she started for the front door, then remembered her vow to never step on the threshold again. Turning around, she raced toward the back, her eyes blurred by tears.

Angrily wiping the moisture from her face, she paced quickly to Mrs. Butterfield's home, paying little attention to where she placed her feet. At one point she stepped into a deep pit—the imprint of a British cannon ball—twisted her ankle, and fell. She cried in pain and fought back an expletive. Sitting in the middle of the road, she gave full vent to her tears, grateful at least that no one was there to see her graceless fall.

After a moment, she pushed herself up from the road and wiped the dirt from her apparel. Gingerly taking a step, she winced at the pain in her ankle.

Pushing onward, she forced herself to ignore the discomfort and walk more carefully along Concord Road. She knew it would be a long time before the marks of battle could be erased from this place.

It took her several moments longer to arrive at Mrs. Butterfield's home. The woman seemed more anxious than ever to see her.

"I vow, Betsy, I'm so thankful you're here. I do believe Edward's infection is worsening."

Betsy shook her head in confusion. "Edward?"

"Aye, the lieutenant. His name is Edward."

"I see."

It had never occurred to Betsy that he had a name other than "Lieutenant Hall."

Or "enemy soldier." Or "blaggart."

Betsy's thoughts shocked even herself.

Pray, what's happening to me? God forgive me.

Mrs. Butterfield continued. "I've sent a message to the army doctor in Boston. Perhaps he should see him. Perhaps there's more I should be doing."

"The army doctor? Coming here?" Betsy gulped. "How does he cross the barricade at Charlestown?"

"He and the nurses are allowed to enter carrying a flag of truce. 'Tis permitted by our militia for acts of compassion."

Betsy's astonishment dropped her jaw. "I see." But she was baffled.

Our troops allow acts of compassion?

Mercy did not reside in her heart anymore. Certainly not toward the enemy.

As if reading Betsy's thoughts, Mrs. Butterfield touched her arm. "You know, Betsy, we all share common blood. This man is our brother."

Betsy stiffened and tightened her jaw as the woman continued.

"Dissension between brothers is as old as Cain and Abel, Betsy. War is the result of the evil in men's hearts, yet God desires we be merciful."

Betsy's eyes rested on the floor, and she shifted her legs uncomfortably. Ignoring the woman's words, Betsy stared with stubborn determination at her neighbor. "How can I help you today, Mrs. Butterfield?"

The older woman inhaled deeply. "I have been up all night, changing linens, giving him laudanum. Pray, could you stay with Edward whilst I rest?" Mrs. Butterfield leaned against the wall, and Betsy feared she would sink to the floor right then and there.

"Of course, Mrs. Butterfield."

The woman smiled, squeezed Betsy's arm, and headed for her bedchamber.

With weighted legs, Betsy limped toward the room where the soldier lay. She winced when she moved her ankle just so but was relieved she had not injured herself more severely. Arriving at Lieutenant Hall's room, she was shocked by the new odor that met her nostrils. It was definitely an infection.

She tried to tiptoe in, despite her inflamed ankle. When the officer opened his eyes, she halted her efforts to move unobtrusively.

"Good day, Miss Russell." His voice rasped.

"Good day, sir."

She noticed the moisture on his face as she walked closer to him. His eyes were glazed with pain. The lieutenant lay on his uninjured side, and Mrs. Butterfield had propped pillows under his damaged arm.

"May I get you anything?" Her eyebrow furrowed. "You seem to be in more pain today."

"Aye. I am. Please … the laudanum."

She poured a generous portion into the small vial. When she held up the bottle, she saw it was nearly empty. "I hope the doctor brings more with him from Boston."

"The doctor?"

"Aye. Mrs. Butterfield has sent for him."

He closed his eyes.

Bringing him the cup of medicine, she walked closer to him.

"Are you able to swallow whilst lying on your side?"

"Aye. Mrs. Butterfield told me I must … adjust my body so as not to get sores."

Not that it matters in the end.

Betsy bit her lip. "I see. Here."

She held the cup to his trembling, anxious lips, and he swallowed the liquid eagerly. The patient gasped, then breathed with difficulty for a few moments until he seemed to recover from the effort.

After a short time, he relaxed. She returned the empty vial to the table. "Would you care for any ale?" Betsy surprised herself. She had never offered him sustenance before.

"Perhaps a small quaff." He smiled, then winced.

"Perhaps I should place it in the vial as well."

He met her eyes. "That is what Mrs. Butterfield does."

She filled the small container with ale from a nearby tankard, spilling a small amount on the table. Reaching for a linen cloth to mop it up, she twisted her ankle again and winced. Ignoring the discomfort, she limped to his bedside and held the ale to his thirsty lips. He swallowed it in one gulp.

Smiling somewhat groggily, he jested, "Just like being at a tavern." He started to laugh but coughed instead. She reached out to touch his arm, then pulled away.

"Are you all right?"

After his spasms of coughing ended, he gave a wry grin. "Aye, splendid."

His obvious sarcasm brought a slight smile to her face.

He held her eyes. "You should smile more often. It becomes you."

Ignoring his compliment, Betsy turned and walked carefully toward the chair to sit down. She picked up *Pilgrim's Progress*, feigning interest in the words that, at the moment, seemed as meaningless as riddles in a foreign tongue. She could feel his eyes upon her, but she refused to look at him.

"How did you hurt your ankle?"

Her head lifted in surprise. "How ... never mind."

"It is obvious you have hurt yourself since I saw you last."

Betsy set her jaw. "If you must know, I tripped in a hole on the road. A hole blasted open by one of *your* cannons."

Silence. She spent several moments trying to focus on the familiar passages in *Pilgrim's Progress*, but his presence unnerved her.

"I regret the news of your father."

Betsy whipped her head up and glared at the lieutenant. "What do you know of my father?" She wanted to wound him with the fiery rage she hoped showed in her eyes.

"Mrs. Butterfield told me what happened. I am sorry."

"Sorry? 'Tis too late for regrets, sir. They butchered my father as if he were a pig." Her voice trembled from her fury. "He was an old man—a crippled old man." Tears poured down her cheeks. "'Twas not enough they shot him twice. Then they stabbed him with their bayonets over and over." She could not go on. Betsy covered her mouth, suddenly afraid she would awaken Mrs. Butterfield in the next room.

Wiping her tears away, she glanced at the officer. Dumbfounded, she observed tears rolling onto his pillow.

Neither spoke a word for what seemed an eternity.

Betsy struggled to regain control of her emotions. As she wiped at her face with fierce strokes, she sniffed loudly. Grabbing her apron, she dried the rest of the moisture. When she finally had the courage to face the man again, she said something she never thought she would say to the enemy.

"Forgive my outburst. I know 'twas not your bayonet that killed him, sir."

"No." The man's voice whispered. "But 'twas my army that did so."

Glancing toward the window, he looked off into the distance. "It's no fortunate fate to be the second son." He sniffed with disgust. "My older brother received the manor. I received a post in the army."

Betsy's swollen eyes narrowed. *This bloody back has a heart?*

She shook herself from her stupor. "You had no choice?"

"No. It is what is expected. You do what fate commands."

"I see." Betsy understood expectations well. "So you think 'tis fate that weaves your destiny?"

"Yes." He paused. "I suppose it was never my fate to marry Emmaline, either." A few trickles flowed down his face, glistening in the sunlight. He squinted his eyes and then shut them.

"So, you had to leave Emmaline in England?"

He drew in a deep but slow breath. "Yes. We were to marry—that is, until the war began. I did not ... I did not wish to leave her with perhaps a child on the way to raise alone. She begged me to marry her, but I would not do that to her." More tears. "Now, I wish I had. I wish I had even one night to share in the pleasure of her. To have the memory of her sweetness."

Betsy's eyes widened. To her surprise, her own tears flowed, but they were not for her own grief. She cried for Emmaline. And for Edward.

There is so much I do not understand.

She sat there for a moment, struggling to sort through her feelings. But before she could say anything, he drifted off into a drugged slumber.

Bowing her head, she wept.

God, please forgive me. I've been so filled with hatred. I have scorned the king's men. Please, God, show me how to love my enemy when the wounds from their swords have pierced my heart so deeply. Show me how to forgive.

*   *   *

A loud knock at the front door startled Betsy from her nap. Sitting up, she rubbed her tear-encrusted eyes and saw the sun had moved since her last recollection.

It must be the doctor come from Boston.

Rising with great effort, her sore ankle announced itself with her first step. She proceeded more cautiously. Yawning, she opened the door expecting to see the surgeon accompanied by armed militia. Instead, she gasped at the sight of a hooded man. Pushing his way indoors, he slammed the door shut.

"Where's the bloody-back?"

Her heart raced and her breath caught. It was difficult to answer the man with such a parched throat.

"What do you want?" She did not recognize her own voice.

Wielding a long hunting knife, the disguised ruffian held it in front of her face. "I want to thrust this through his evil heart, that's what."

"You cannot do that, sir. He is dying as it is. Do not imagine that this wrongful deed will be allowed."

He grabbed her arm forcefully. "I'll make this be 'allowed,' miss. Show me where he is."

Who is he? His voice seems familiar but he disguises it! Panic raced through her.

"I shall not show you where he is, sir. You must leave!"

"Then I'll find him myself. And you will accompany me." Pulling her with him, the frightening, hooded figure began searching each room.

She tried pulling back on his arm. "No! Do not do this."

She searched her pocket for the knife that Mr. Watson had given her so many months before. Using her free hand to maneuver the weapon out of the sewing folder—difficult with one hand—she resisted the man's efforts to reach the lieutenant's bedchamber. But Betsy had left the chamber door open, facilitating the patient's discovery by the intruder.

"So here's the bloody-back."

The murderous attacker dropped her arm and tramped toward the bed. With the man's back to her, Betsy used this opportunity to finally free the small hunting knife from her folder and pocket. Dropping the sheath on the floor, she raced toward the bed, stepping in between him and the patient.

Hiding her weapon behind her so he would not grab it, she glared into the man's covered face. "Stand back, sir." With trembling fingers, she manipulated the handle of the blade, preparing to plunge it under his ribs and upward, just as Mr. Watson had taught her.

Her stance confused the intruder at first, but then he ignored her. He reached to push her aside, but she gripped the bedding behind her with her free hand.

God help me!

Already in motion to defend her patient, her knife-wielding hand halted at the sharp voice of Mrs. Butterfield in the doorway.

"Only cowards would kill a dying man."

Betsy inhaled sharply, not knowing what the intruder would do. Her erratic pulse elicited spots in front of her eyes. She could not see his face for the disguise, but she saw his knife slowly lower.

Mrs. Butterfield stomped across the wooden floor and grabbed the man away from Betsy. "Get out!" The woman skewered the man with her eyes. She stepped aside, allowing him to exit.

The front door slammed shut.

Mrs. Butterfield put her arms around Betsy. "Are you all right, Betsy. He did'na hurt you, did he?"

"No." Betsy looked at the knife in her hand and burst into tears. She opened her grasp and let it fall to the floor, then covered her eyes. Mrs. Butterfield embraced her as she trembled uncontrollably. After several moments, Betsy stepped back and remembered the lieutenant. Turning toward him she placed her hand on his uninjured arm.

"Are you all right?"

He smiled weakly. "Yes." He swallowed with difficulty. "Thank you."

He winced with obvious pain. How long had he been without the narcotic? Betsy had lost all track of time.

Mrs. Butterfield hurried to pour the remaining drops of laudanum into the vial. Betsy took it from her hand. "I shall give it to him, Mrs. Butterfield."

"Thank you, Betsy. I shall grab my firelock and wait by the door, lest we have any more 'visitors.'"

Turning to leave, she looked back. "You did well, Betsy."

Betsy's lips trembled. "I nearly killed a man."

Mrs. Butterfield's eyes narrowed. "'Twould have been just, Betsy. In God's eyes, and mine."

The woman left the room, and Betsy brought the vial of medicine to the grimacing patient. He struggled to swallow but imbibed it all.

He looked at her in confusion. "Why? Why did you not let that man end my life?"

"I could not let him murder you, no matter what he thought you had done. Not even an enemy soldier."

"He had a knife. You could have been killed."

She stared at the patient in the bed for a long moment, contemplating what had just occurred.

"T'would not have mattered, if I had died doing the right thing." She paused. "If I did not do the right thing, it would mean something inside my soul had died. Nothing is worth that. Not even my life."

She walked to the chair on unsteady legs. This time she found another book to read. She opened up the Bible—words of comfort to solace her and words of life to fill her soul.

18

'Tis the irony of war that the very weapon meant to save me from my enemy was instead the means to save my enemy. I shall never understand God's ways.

~ Diary of Betsy Russell, 26 April 1775

APRIL 27, 1775
THURSDAY MORNING

Betsy spent all of Wednesday helping her mother plant the spring garden. She returned to the Butterfield home on Thursday, and bewilderment seized her when she discovered a stranger on the premises—an efficient-looking woman of maturity who was likely as old as Betsy's mother.

Mrs. Butterfield appeared rested while she explained the woman's presence. "She's a nurse the doctor sent from Boston. He was not able to come, their hospitals crammed full of soldiers and all. The nurse has been quite helpful with cleaning and such. And she brought more laudanum with her."

"Oh." Betsy glanced at the floor. "Perhaps you do not need me then?" She tried to hide the disappointment in her voice.

Mrs. Butterfield smiled. "Well, you need not feel obligated, but I must tell you, the first words from Edward's mouth were, 'That lovely Miss Russell will still come, will she not'?" Mrs. Butterfield smiled. "He thinks quite highly of his heroine."

"Heroine?" Betsy self-consciously twirled a loose strand of hair that escaped her cap. "I vow, his fever is affecting his senses."

"It does not take a fever to make a man notice a lass as fair as yourself. And a brave one." Her smile faded, and she looked into the distance. "Sometimes, I do not understand the way of it."

"The way of what?" Betsy tilted her head.

Mrs. Butterfield gazed at Betsy. "The way of life ... and death." She sighed. "Come. Let us see what's to be done for him."

Betsy followed the woman to his bedchamber. Edward Hall's state startled Betsy, and she gasped. Although she knew he was dying, in the two days since she'd seen him, his appearance had deteriorated. His sunken eyes appeared darker while his skin paled. And the scent of infection was stronger than ever. Betsy struggled to retain the meal within her stomach.

"Good day, sir."

He saw her and smiled. "Good day, miss."

His words stuck together due to the dryness of his mouth. He did not seem to notice. Or if he did, he did not express embarrassment about his speech.

He watched her walk toward him.

"Your ankle, it is well?"

"Aye, much better."

Why is he asking how I am?

"How do you fare, sir?"

"Splendid." He tried to laugh but coughed at the effort.

Without asking him if he needed it, she dispensed a brown liquid from a tankard into the pewter vial. She sniffed the unfamiliar offering. "Rum?"

"Aye, the doctor wishes him to have it as much as he likes." Mrs. Butterfield tried to smile, but her efforts were thwarted by a sudden welling of tears. She turned away as if to straighten out some pillows.

Betsy knew the rum was to help with the increasing pain, the final misery that would lead to his death. Swallowing back her own tears, she sniffed and brought the drink to the patient.

"Here is your sustenance, sir."

His trembling hand grabbed the vial and her fingers as she guided it to his mouth. She did all the work as he struggled to affix his lips to the cup but allowed him to attempt to help. Her heart clenched at his ineffective yet commendable efforts.

Mrs. Butterfield excused herself from the room. Betsy was left alone with the dying man.

"Is there anything else I can get for you, Lieutenant Hall?"

"Yes." He swallowed forcefully. "Could you get some paper and be my scribe? I wish to write a letter, but somehow my hand will not cooperate." He smiled sadly.

"Of course. Let me find some for you."

It took just a few moments to gather writing supplies from Mrs. Butterfield: quill, ink, parchment, and talc to dry the ink. Betsy set up the writing implements on the small table where the books were kept. She dunked the tip of the goose quill into a bottle of ink and looked up.

"I am ready, sir."

At first she thought the officer had fallen asleep. Soon it was obvious he was trying to decide what to say. He spoke the words as clearly as he could, although painstakingly slow:

> *My dearest Emmaline,*
> *I pray you will forgive me for not writing*
> *for such a long while, but I have been somewhat*
> *incapacitated.*
> *My dearest love, it is my great misfortune and*
> *sadness to tell you that I have been wounded. It is not*
> *likely that I shall recover. Please forgive me for not*
> *staying out of the line of fire as you so instructed at our*
> *last meeting.*

Betsy was not sure how she would complete this missive. Her tears threatened to blend with the ink as she tried desperately to stroke out legible words. His deep affection for his Emmaline was dictated with such ardent detail that Betsy blushed at his passion for this woman whose body and soul had captured his favor and admiration. Struggling to complete this most personal—and final—letter to his Emmaline, Betsy laboriously finished the most difficult letter she had ever inscribed.

I love you from the depths of my heart and soul.
I pray that you will find another that loves you even half
as much as I.
Your most humble and faithful servant,
Edward Hall, 1ˢᵗ Lieutenant
His Majesty's Royal 43ʳᵈ Regiment

Betsy sprinkled some talc on the parchment, hoping the dry powder would absorb all the ink, as well as her tears.

Carefully folding the parchment after it dried, Betsy pulled the thin ribbon off her mobcap and wrapped it around the very private letter to keep it from being easily opened. She tied the knot extra tight.

"There, Lieutenant Hall. Your letter to Emmaline." She handed it to him.

Instead of taking it, he folded her fingers around the tied parchment. "You keep it. Send it with my body back to Boston. My general will see it safely to Emmaline."

Betsy's mouth opened. "Nonsense, sir. I can send it—"

"No, Miss Russell. Please, do as I ask."

Betsy wanted to protest such a request, but she could not bring herself to argue with a dying man. "I shall do as you ask, sir."

"And please ..."

"Yes, sir?" She swallowed, wishing she could run away somewhere and hide—anywhere—just to be alone.

"Miss, please call me Edward. I have dictated to you ... my most personal, intimate thoughts ... about the woman I love." He smiled weakly. "I do believe we should ... at least be able to call each other ... by our Christian names."

Betsy glanced at the floor and felt heat rise in her cheeks.

"You are truly lovely ... when you blush, Miss Russell."

Her cheeks now flamed. Looking away, she relented. "Very well, Edward. You may call me Betsy."

He grinned widely, his gums bright red from fever.

"Ah ... friends at last. It will be ... so much more comfortable ... when you ... are changing my bed linens."

Betsy's mouth trembled. "Please do not say that, Edward."

He looked at her, capturing her gaze with his darkened eyes. "Betsy, it will ... all be well at the end. Your words the other day—about the life in your soul—brought the light of conviction ... to my own heart. I have been searching ... my own soul ... and found it lacking. Rather ... God revealed to me I was lacking. I wonder ... could you find it in your heart ... to read to me from the Gospels?"

Her lips quivered, her mind a jumbled symphony of emotions. "Of course, Edward."

She walked over to the table and picked up the Bible. This time, she slid the chair across the floor and settled it next to her patient.

Opening to the Gospel of John, she read out loud.

"In the beginning was the Word and the Word was with God, and the Word was God."

As she continued to read to him, a look of peace relaxed across his features. It was a peace that Betsy knew transcended loyalties to nations and demonstrated they were subjects before one king—the King of Kings.

19

*I've been contemplating Edward's sentiments for Emmaline. Could I
ever imagine receiving such a missive from Amos? Nay, his affection for
me was to please himself. Edward's thoughts were for his Emmaline's
benefit and well-being. Did I e'er think I would learn so much about
love from my enemy?*

~ Diary of Betsy Russell, 29 April 1775

APRIL 30, 1775
SABBATH DAY

They all knew that Edward Hall's call to eternity was imminent. The
fact that he was still her enemy in war no longer clouded Betsy's
judgment of the man as a human being created by God. Her main duty
was to help him through his suffering and try not to think about his
impending demise.

Betsy encouraged Mrs. Butterfield to attend Sabbath services. She
knew the older woman needed spiritual sustenance. Mrs. Butterfield's
life had been turned upside down by this unexpected intrusion into
her home. Betsy chose to immerse herself in Scripture and read to the
lieutenant when he desired to hear.

The nurse from Boston spoke to Betsy as she brewed coffee over
the hearth.

"Is there no tea to be had here in the countryside?" The woman's
large features expressed her annoyance.

"Nay, Mrs. Lambert. We drink coffee here in Menotomy. Would
you care for a cup?" Betsy smiled graciously.

"I suppose." The woman shook her head slowly. "I do not know
how ye rebels tolerate such a drink."

Betsy smiled, not revealing her own preference for black tea. There were some things in life more important than a favorite beverage, she had learned. Considering the critical state of Edward Hall, Betsy mused that missing tea was a trivial discomfort.

"'Tis a wonder poor Lieutenant Hall still hangs on," Betsy said. She set her cup of coffee down, acutely aware of the bitter taste.

"Aye, 'tis a sadness for the poor lad to be sure. These young ones— they often cling to life longer than we old ones."

Betsy shivered.

Must I watch the man die? Can I bear it? God, help me to be stronger than I feel.

Focusing on Mrs. Lambert, Betsy shook away her thoughts of his impending death.

"I suppose 'tis more difficult to depart this world when it seems too soon for the letting go of one's spirit." She stood up. "I'll go see if he needs anything." She did not wish Mrs. Lambert to see her tears.

Tiptoeing to the bedchamber, Betsy braced herself for Edward's restlessness. He'd been unable to find a comfortable position, and it made his travail even more difficult to observe.

"Edward, can I get you anything?" She placed a hand on his arm.

He jerked it away as though it pained him. He then opened his sunken eyes, glazed and unseeing. "Who ... who is that with you?"

Betsy turned around, thinking Mrs. Lambert had followed her. She reasoned the woman was still in the main room, because she heard the clatter of pewter plates.

"There is no one with me, Edward." She kept her voice low.

He narrowed his eyes. "Yes, there's ... a young woman with you." He shivered uncontrollably and turned, moaning in pain.

Betsy turned around again and saw no one. She puzzled over Edward's remark, but fear did not overwhelm her.

As he turned, the bandage on his shoulder slipped, partly revealing black skin underneath. Betsy cringed at the mortified tissue, dying even before his body had a chance to. She put her hand to her mouth to control her shuddering.

Pulling her hand away, she straightened her back and strode with purpose toward the bottle of laudanum. Mrs. Butterfield had said he hadn't had a dose since early morning, and Mrs. Lambert had arisen from her slumber only recently.

As she measured out the medicine, Betsy heard the bell at the meetinghouse ring for the service. Every time she heard that tolling, it reminded her of the night the king's soldiers marched through their village.

Will that ringing ever again feel like a summons to a peaceful service on Sabbath? Will it always send alarm through my spirit?

She prayed it would not.

Mrs. Lambert joined them. "Ah, I see you've got the laudanum ready. Good, lass."

They had been through this cooperative effort before. Mrs. Lambert strode toward Edward and gently lifted his head with her strong arms while Betsy held the vial to his lips.

"Edward, take a sip." He always obeyed. With the same care as before, Mrs. Lambert lowered the man's head down. He was now propped up on several pillows to help his labored breathing. At times, he strained to take in his gasping breaths, especially when he was somewhat alert.

Opening his eyes, his gaze roamed around with uncertainty. He whispered incomprehensively until his eyes rested on Betsy's face. His expression emanated surprise. "Emmaline?"

Betsy's pulse raced with anxiety and confusion. "No, Edward. 'Tis Betsy."

He seemed more bewildered and agitated. "Emmaline?"

Looking at Mrs. Lambert, Betsy's eyes sought direction from the experienced nurse. She replied, "T'will not be an offense to be Emmaline for the moment."

The nurse turned away, and Betsy heard her sniff.

Betsy turned back to Edward and drew closer so he could see her. "Yes, Edward."

He smiled weakly. "Emmaline." She reached for his hand and he clung to it tightly. Closing his eyes, he relaxed and smiled. "Emmaline." Soon he slept again.

Betsy's hand held his for the rest of the morning. When Mrs. Butterfield returned from Sabbath service, Betsy looked at her with dried tears on her face.

"He thought I was Emmaline." Betsy burst into fresh tears as she released his hand onto the bed covers.

Mrs. Butterfield rushed toward her and embraced the sobbing young woman. Betsy cried for Edward, for her father, and for her troubled nation struggling for freedom. She wept for all the sons and daughters who were now fatherless, the parents now childless, the lovers now left with empty arms.

Her arms felt the emptiest of all.

WEDNESDAY, MAY 3, 1775

Edward entered eternity early in the day.

None of his caregivers were surprised. Indeed, they were all amazed he had lingered a fortnight. Near the end, the women prayed for relief from his suffering. Their prayers were finally answered at dawn.

Mrs. Lambert sent a note to General Gage, who arranged transport of the body back to Boston for return to his homeland. Edward would finally get to go home. The sad thought was little consolation to Betsy as she stared at the letter she held—his final declaration of love to Emmaline.

Betsy watched the wagon pull up in front of Mrs. Butterfield's home. A gathering of curious—some angry—onlookers from Menotomy stood off to the side, watching what was an intriguing ceremony of sorts.

Edward's body was wrapped in a clean sheet and laid in the back of a horse-drawn wagon. Two armed officers of the militia and several provincial soldiers, all on horseback, accompanied the funeral procession. Before they left, Betsy hurried to one of the officers that she recognized from the Committee of Safety.

"Dr. Warren." She shielded her eyes from the sun as she stared up at the soldier on horseback.

"Aye, miss?"

Suddenly self-conscious, she felt everyone's eyes focused upon her. Remembering her promise to Edward emboldened her. "Dr. Warren, I have here a letter for a friend of this soldier. He had me inscribe it for him before he died."

Handing the beribboned parchment to the officer, she watched him read the address. Placing the missive in his pocket, he patted it firmly with his hand. "I'll see this note gets to the proper recipient." He looked carefully at Betsy. "You are Miss Russell, are you not?"

Startled by his recognition, she replied, "Aye, sir. Jason Russell was my father."

His intense gaze unnerved her.

"Yet ye tended a dying enemy soldier—even after your father was so mercilessly torn from this life?"

He scowled, but she refused to be intimidated.

"Aye, sir. My father did not allow his passion for freedom to interfere with his obedience to God. He used to tell me, 'Betsy, 'tis imperative to forgive. 'Tis the Lord's command.'" She drew in a ragged breath and tears welled in her eyes. "I pray I can always honor my father's wishes, as well as the desires of my Heavenly Father."

A small smile emerged on Dr. Warren's crinkled face. "So you have, Miss Russell. So you have." Tipping his tricorne hat to her, he patted the pocket containing the letter to Emmaline. "I'll deliver this letter without fail."

"Thank you, sir." Betsy stepped away from the horses and watched the military procession disappear into the distance.

She stood there for several moments before comforting arms embraced her. Her mother looked her in the eye. "You make your father proud, Betsy."

Fatigue overwhelmed her as tears rolled down her face. Nearly two weeks of tending to the dying while learning so much of life had exhausted Betsy.

Her brother, Thomas, sauntered to her side from the curious crowd that still gathered to watch the procession. Wrapping his arms around her, he gently squeezed her shoulder. "Let's go home, Betsy."

They walked together to the Russell home in reverent silence.

20

Pumpkin had a litter of kittens today. 'Tis amazing such small creatures can bring a glimpse of joy to my heart. Perhaps we shall keep a small one—the boy kitten with dark hair. I shall call him "Edward."

~ Diary of Betsy Russell, 3 June 1775

EARLY JUNE, 1775

Life in Menotomy Village would never be the same. Betsy realized that she would never be the same, either.

As difficult as these tragedies had been, she had survived. She now understood that survival of integrity—indeed of one's character and faith—was the most enduring quality of all. The body would eventually die, but the soul was eternal.

Betsy determined to bring flowers once a week to the graves of the buried British soldiers who had died in Menotomy. There were at least forty of them.

Occasionally she would meet Mrs. Butterfield at their graves. The two women spoke little about these visits, just shared a smile and the common belief that everyone's life should be remembered and respected. The king's soldiers had been unceremoniously buried against the wall where the slaves were interred.

Betsy also placed some flowers on the grave where their slave, Katy, had been buried. And then Sarah's grave. Her heart ached for her friend. *I will always miss her. There is so much I wish to share.*

But most of all, Betsy desperately missed her father. Each day she strode the hundred rods to the burial ground to stand by his grave for a few moments. Today she brought him freshly-bloomed lavender.

Today there was also news she felt compelled to share. Though his physical ears could no longer hear, perhaps his spirit could. Betsy felt better for the telling of it, even if her words disappeared into the wind. She always felt closer to him here, where his remains lay.

"Father, I must tell you, you were right about Tess." She swallowed and adjusted her bonnet in the early morning sun. "Noah found her at dawn. She must have ... she must have just stopped breathing. We did not know." She wiped away a few tears. "Her calf was beside her. She is a strong and fine young one. She was near-weaned, so Noah brought her out with the other cows. They will look after her."

She set the sprigs of lavender down. "The flowers are early this year, Father. I know lavender was your favorite.

"Thomas helped Noah plant the corn this year. You would be proud of Noah. He's become quite the responsible lad. No more dragging him from bed every morning." She chuckled. "He still practices shooting the marks. I think he'll be a fine hunter." Her expression darkened. "I pray he need never use his skill for war."

Betsy inhaled a deep breath. "Jason has joined the militia in New Hampshire, Father. I am relieved that Thomas will stay here in Menotomy. I could not bear for him to be in battle again. I try not to fear for our troops gathering near Boston. I know there'll be more fighting soon. I pray 'twill be finished after this." She bit her lip. "I miss you so."

Betsy pulled out her kerchief and blew her nose. As she wiped her face, she heard the clomping of footsteps behind her, marching in time.

The militia!

A few officers on horseback accompanied the foot soldiers. As they neared the burying ground, one of the officers commanded the infantry to halt and salute.

In unison, the company of troops faced the grave where Betsy stood, and they saluted. Another verbal command drew the men back in formation, facing straight ahead on the road to Boston. The company drummer offered a steady beat and the men kept time as they headed east on Concord Road.

Betsy startled to see one of the officers guide his horse slowly toward her. Her eyes widened as he got closer, and he pulled the reins to stop the animal. Dismounting, the provincial soldier, handsome in his blue wool uniform, stepped slowly toward her, removing his tricorne hat.

"Please forgive the intrusion, miss. Our unit just wished to pay respects to the brave soldiers of Menotomy who shed their blood here. Up in York County, their bravery is being hailed with high esteem."

Betsy's mouth opened and heat flushed her cheeks.

"I … I am astonished at your presence, sir." She stared at a sprig of lavender that she twirled in her hands.

The man stared with focused eyes at Betsy.

She shifted her feet.

"Aye, miss. 'Tis well known in Maine, New Hampshire— everywhere—what happened here that day. More died in your village than any other town."

She turned sideways and blinked, attempting to hide her emotions. "Aye. 'Twas a day I'll not soon forget."

He pointed to the large area of freshly turned earth. Weeds now covered the dirt, along with Betsy's lavender. "Do you have kin here, miss?" His voice was soft and sympathetic.

"Aye. My father. They killed him on our doorstep." Tears rolled down her cheeks, despite her attempts to hold them back.

He cleared his throat. "I am sorry."

Silence.

"Miss, please forgive my lack of manners. I am Corporal Jotham Webber. Our militia unit is on its way to Boston. More troops are gathering everyday. Thousands are rallying for the patriot cause, now. We shall win this war, wait and see." He paused. "Your father will not have died in vain."

Wiping the tears from her eyes, she attempted a smile. "Thank you, Corporal Webber." She glanced up, overcoming her shyness. "I am Miss Elizabeth Russell."

He grinned and bowed slightly. "Pleased to make your acquaintance, Miss Russell." His ruddy face was a stark contrast to his pale, long hair, which was pulled back in a black ribbon. The woolen coat of his uniform appeared newly made.

"Someone has sewn you a fine uniform, Corporal Webber."

I wonder if 'twas his wife? She kept herself from biting her lip.

He looked downward self-consciously. "Aye. My mother would not allow her son to go to battle in his hunting shirt. 'Twould not have mattered to me."

Relief! But perhaps he has a lady waiting for him? Why would he not, so handsome is he? She shook her head. *Stop it, Betsy!*

"Well, 'tis quite handsome." Blushing with embarrassment, she was horrified at her own boldness. "I mean, 'twill serve you well."

"Thank you, miss."

Looking up at the man who now stood just a few feet away, she met his eyes. "I shall pray for you, Corporal Webber."

He seemed unable to speak for a moment, but his expression melted her heart with warmth.

"Thank you, Miss Russell. I am truly grateful." He looked suddenly at his unit that was fast disappearing up the road. "I'd best rejoin the troops." He seemed reluctant to leave. "I ... I wonder, Miss Russell, might I write to you? Please, forgive me being so forward."

Heat rose in Betsy's cheeks again as she looked at the ground. She lifted her gaze. "Aye, you may write to me, Corporal Webber."

"Please, call me Jotham. I know we've only just met ..." His voice trailed off.

She wanted to laugh but did not wish to embarrass him. "I shall be happy to sign my letters to Corporal Jotham." Her eyes teased him.

He exhaled. "Thank you, miss. May I address you as Elizabeth?" She watched him swallow.

She paused, then said as seriously as she could, "Nay, you may not, sir."

His expression fell. "I see." He started to put his hat back on, but she touched his arm lightly.

"You may not call me Elizabeth. That is my given name. You may call me 'Betsy'—like all my friends do."

His white teeth shone in his sunburned face. "Aye. Betsy it is, then."

She removed her hand from his arm, but he impulsively grabbed it for a moment and squeezed her fingers tenderly. "I look forward to the day I see you again, Betsy." As Jotham climbed into his saddle, Betsy noticed his coat flip to the side.

His sheath is empty.

Grabbing the rein, Betsy's eyes widened. "Wait. Your sheath. You have no knife."

His lips pressed together in annoyance. "Nay, I lost it night before last."

Rummaging in her pocket, she withdrew her sewing folder. She released the rein she had been holding and pulled the knife out of its silk sheath. Holding it by the blade, she handed it up to Jotham. "Here."

His eyes narrowed. "Pray, what is this? And in a sewing folder?"

She shielded her eyes from the sun as she looked up at him. "'Tis a long tale, to be certain."

"Do you not need this?" He looked it over carefully.

"You shall need it far more than I." Pausing, she inhaled deeply and stood as tall as she was able. "I no longer fear death, but resolve to trust in God for my future and my life. And I pray that this weapon, which has been forged in fire, will help bring you safely through the fires of battle, Corporal Webber." She smiled. "Jotham."

"Thank you, Betsy." Doffing his hat, he smiled and pulled his mount back toward the road.

Betsy called after him. "Jotham, where is the militia going?"

He stopped briefly. "A place called Bunker Hill." He coaxed his mare into a canter to catch up with his unit that was now out of sight.

"Godspeed, Jotham. Godspeed." Her voice carried to him on the wind.

Afterword

Corporal Jotham Webber returned from war safely. He and Betsy Russell married in 1778 while the war was still being fought. They had their first child in Menotomy Village, then moved to Mason, New Hampshire, the same town where her nephew, Josiah, lived. In all, Betsy and Jotham had nine children.

Old Samuel Whittemore survived his wounds from the British assault. He lived to the age of ninety-eight.

Noah and his mother continued to reside together in the Russell home. Elizabeth Russell died in 1786 at the age of sixty-five. She is buried next to her husband, Jason, in the Old Burying Ground. In 1782, Noah married Eunice Bemis of Watertown, and they raised their five children in the family home.

Noah's daughter, Lydia, married Thomas Teel in 1814, and they raised a large family there. For many years, the residence was called the Teel House.

Over the years, various additions changed the look of the Russell House slightly, but the original framework and construction is still intact. There are still several bullet holes visible in the entryway to the cellar, the hallway, and the downstairs chamber. The home's original floorboards, which were covered with blood following the 1775 battle, were replaced in 1863.

The house, now known as the Jason Russell House, is open as a museum and is operated by the Arlington Historical Society in Arlington, Massachusetts.

Author's Note

When I was a young girl living in Arlington, Massachusetts, my brother and I walked by the Jason Russell House on the way to school. Like most older brothers, Bob enjoyed scaring me. As we approached the house on the corner, he'd say in his most frightening tone, "There's blood on the floor in there, you know."

I was a bit unnerved, but mostly I was curious.

What had happened there? And why was there a sign that said it was a historical landmark?

I knew there must be a story. But I didn't learn—until I became an adult—the full depth of the tragedy that occurred there.

The real sadness of the tale was how personal it was for the family that lived in that house: Jason Russell—husband, father, and grandfather—was murdered right on his doorstep by British soldiers. He was a fourth-generation colonial farmer living in a small village in Massachusetts. He was old and lame. And they killed him mercilessly.

It all happened on the first day of the American Revolution, the same date that the battles of Lexington and Concord occurred. In fact, more soldiers—both American and British—died in Menotomy Village (now called Arlington) on that day than all the other towns between Concord and Boston. Yet history books skim right over the trail of bloodshed that spilled on the earth in Menotomy. The story beckoned to be told.

And what better way to help a reader or student of history understand the depth of the details than by taking the point of view of one of the people who lived through that day and turn it into a novel? History could then come alive, in all its painful truth, and reveal to us all lessons that are as old as time. For example, war is sometimes necessary but always horrible.

We all understand the tragedy of war from a distance. But what about those who heard every scream and burst of gunfire? What about the women and children that waged their own war against fear? I decided to write the story from the point of view of Jason Russell's then eighteen-year-old daughter, Betsy. *Fields of the Fatherless* became her story.

In *The Boston Campaign, April 1775 – March 1776* by Victor Brooks, he wrote, "The 'Battle of Menotomy' became the most brutal engagement of the day as house-to-house and room-to-room fighting resulted in Regulars and militiamen clubbing and bayoneting one another, pistols flashing, men swinging tomahawks and hunting knives and dozens of casualties on each side." It was the ultimate horror of an already horrible day of fighting.

Many of the incidents depicted in this historical novel actually occurred. Even the simple scene of Anna brewing tea for a headache just before the neighborhood committee man showed up. That incident was documented in Benjamin and William Cutter's, *History of the Town of Arlington, Massachusetts*.

Other stories in this novel were gleaned from Samuel Abbott Smith's *West Cambridge 1775*, published by The Arlington Historical Society.

The tragedy of young Mrs. Fessenden, who was holding her infant when a stray bullet hit her in the eye, sadly did occur.

Some of the scenes depicted in the Prentiss' house of refuge were factual. Rumor did fly that the slaves would rise up against their owners.

And Anna Russell, wife of Thomas Russell, did give birth on that day. Sadly, baby Anna died "soon," the genealogy records indicate. She was, indeed, baptized the Sunday after the battle.

Mother Batherick, who interrupted the Sabbath service in my novel, did in fact have several British soldiers surrender to her while she was pulling dandelions. Her lecture to the terrified soldiers was taken verbatim from accounts of the incident.

Sections of sermons from Reverend Samuel Cooke, a fiery patriot in the pulpit, were also taken from historical accounts.

And Mrs. Butterfield, upon returning from seeking refuge on April 19, 1775, did indeed find a wounded British officer bleeding on her bed. She nursed him for two weeks until he died of his wounds. During the course of his illness, a man did enter Mrs. Butterfield's home, threatening to kill the Redcoat. She held off the murderer by saying that he was a coward for attempting to kill a dying man.

While many of the connecting details of the account—and certainly most of the dialogue and *all* of Betsy's diary entries—are from my writer's imagination, I endeavored to keep as much of the real history alive in this novel as possible.

Today I understand the details of "the blood on the floor," so descriptively brought to my attention by my brother, Bob. And while the original wooden slats that cradled the bodies of twelve patriots in 1775 were removed long ago, the story behind this massacre still lives on.

As well as the knowledge that the men's blood was not shed in vain.

97223952R00077

Made in the USA
Middletown, DE
03 November 2018